Dedicated to two very wonderful people,
my mother and father

D0647454

L.E.O. BRAACK

A Struik All-Colour guide to the

KRUGER NATIONAL PARK

C. STRUIK. CAPE TOWN

C. Struik (Pty) Ltd
Struik House
Oswald Pirow Street
Foreshore
Cape Town
8001

First Edition 1983

Copyright © (text and pictures) L.E.O. Braack

Cover Design by Janice Ashby Studio, Cape Town
Designed by Joanne Simpson, Cape Town
Photoset by McManus Bros (Pty) Ltd, Cape Town
Lithographic Reproduction by Unifoto (Pty) Ltd, Cape Town
Printed and Bound by Mandarin Publishers (Pty) Ltd, Hong Kong

All rights reserved. No part of this publication may be
reproduced, stored in a retrieval system or transmitted, in any
form or by any means, electronic, mechanical, photocopying,
recording or otherwise, without the permission in writing of the
copyright owner.

ISBN 0 86977 142 6

Opposite title page: A lioness stares intently at a distant herd of impala.

Page 8: Elephant, such as this one in the mopane veld near Shingwedzi, remain one of the
prime viewing attractions for visitors to the Park.

Contents

A comprehensive checklist of the main species of flora and fauna to be seen in the Park also serves as an index.

Acknowledgements

It has been a great pleasure compiling this book on an area very dear to me, and I wish to thank the many people who contributed in ways both big and small. Firstly, the National Parks Board for the opportunity and facilities provided me. To Dr Pienaar, who found time in his hard-pressed schedule to read and comment on the manuscript, and to write the foreword. Parts of the manuscript were also read by P. van Wyk, V. de Vos, P. du Plessis, S. Joubert, W. Gertenbach, W. Trollope, T. Dearlove, I. Whyte, I. Espie, H. Jacobson, J. Browne and R. Miller, all of whom offered valuable comments. Many other people, too, provided information or help: to Frans Laubscher, Piet du Plessis, Anthony Hall-Martin, Daryl Mason, Winston Trollope, Caryl Pritchard, Nicky Schoeman, Gina Jarman, Lorna Stanton, Hugo van Niekerk, and all the camp managers and trails rangers, thank you very much indeed. My gratitude also to Tessa Browne, Merle Whyte, Dawn Oelofse, Gail Browne and Maureen Rochat, who typed and retyped, often slaving late at night to meet deadlines. I also acknowledge the help of Ian Espie, Howard Jacobson, and the National Parks Board, in supplying some of the photographs. Finally, to Peter Borchert, Peter Schirmer, and Walther Votteler, all of Struik Publishers, thank you for your diplomacy, skill, guidance, advice, and hard work.

Foreword

Since its beginning, and even before that time, many books, articles and brochures have been written about the Kruger National Park, variously propounding the splendours of its natural fauna and flora and its landscapes, its history and years of achievement as well as relating the lives and anecdotes of its custodians – the people behind the scene, who administer and care for this great wildlife sanctuary.

Never yet, however, has a book been produced by one who was actually born, bred and reared in these wild and untouched realms. Leo Braack, who is the author of this omnibus guide-book to the Kruger Park is such a person, having been born at Skukuza in 1954 of parents who themselves spent many years of their lives in service of the Kruger Park departments of technical services (his father was a mechanician) and tourism (his mother an administration clerk). The profound love of nature of the Braacks runs even more deeply in the family as an elder brother, Harold, is today Warden of the famed Addo Elephant National Park near Port Elizabeth. After his primary and high school days at Skukuza Primary and Belfast High schools, Leo took a degree with entomology as his major subject at the University of Natal, from where he at once returned to the Park to do a postgraduate project on the influence of blow-flies in the transmission of the dreaded animal disease anthrax.

With this background he is eminently qualified to write knowledgeably and with authority on all aspects of the Kruger Park. This is exactly what he has done and his somewhat bulky guide-book 'The All-colour guide to the Kruger National Park' relates at length about the birth and early years of the Kruger Park, the history of development of the Park, and he also deals in detail with the topography, climate, the wealth of flora and fauna as well as other aspects such as the facilities, information services, wilderness trails, travelling hours, general regulations, the various rest-camps and even provides hints on game-viewing and the best routes to follow in order to preclude disappointment.

The scope of the book is exceptionally wide but the style is lively, the information concise but not boring, and for those visitors who wish to buy a single volume that will satisfy all their questions about this intriguing natural wonderland, Leo Braack's 'The All-colour guide to the Kruger National Park' is the obvious choice.

It therefore gives me great pleasure to introduce this well illustrated and valuable guide-book to our visitors. I am convinced that even the briefest perusal will add immensely to the proper planning of their visits and the enjoyment of their stay.

DR U. DE V. PIENAAR
WARDEN: KRUGER NATIONAL PARK, SKUKUZA. AUGUST 1982

The birth . . .

During the pioneer years of the 19th century the eastern Lowveld of the Transvaal was a harsh and inhospitable area few wished to enter. Despite the large herds of animals and fertile ground, the first Voortrekkers passing through in 1837 had no desire to remain in what seemed a God-forsaken land. In the years that followed a few hunters ventured in on horse and ox-cart to periodically plunder the unprotected herds. Many succumbed. Malaria killed men, African horsesickness killed horses, nagana transmitted by tsetse flies killed cattle, and lions killed them all.

Eventually the first settlers arrived, establishing themselves mostly in the foothills of the Drakensberg, well away from the malarious plagues which in summer haunted the low-lying bushveld. During the dry winters parties would descend from places like Barberton, Lydenburg, Pilgrim's Rest, sweeping through the plains to kill indiscriminately for meat, hides, and to satisfy man's long-lingering instinct to hunt. Animals were shot, trapped, or driven from their traditional ranges until only isolated pockets of skittish herds remained.

It was Paul Kruger who eventually saved these dwindling herds. Already in 1884, the president of the Zuid Afrikaansche Republiek had recognized the beauty and value of this much-maligned bushveld and had urged in the Volksraad the need to preserve some of this land. In 1898 after much opposition, he succeeded in officially proclaiming the establishment of a 'Government Reserve' in the Transvaal's east-

Above: Rivers, the life-blood of the Park, are threatened by dam-building and other agricultural practices outside its borders.
◀ Left: Sun rises over a tranquil dam near Skukuza, painting the veld in soft colours.

ern Lowveld. Seen from today's perspective it was not much. The Sabie Game Reserve, as it was to be called, comprised only a strip of land between the Sabie and Crocodile rivers, very small in comparison with the vast Kruger National Park we know today. But more important, vastly more important, it was the beginning of a trend. For the first time an area of worthwhile size had been set aside expressly for conservation, at least on the continent of Africa. Records of the time reflect the antagonism and derision Paul Kruger met when he expressed concern over an area scorned by virtually all. Yet, perhaps, it was the very fact that little value was attached to this region that allowed its proclamation as a protected area.

The uncertain years . . .

Colonel James Stevenson-Hamilton, then a major, entered in July 1902 as the first warden of the Sabie Game Reserve. He arrived with no knowledge of the area, no specific orders or any idea of what his duties were, let alone having been given authority to back up his intended conservation measures.

He stationed himself briefly on the banks of the Crocodile river, familiarizing himself with the land and animals he would come to know so well, but soon moved and settled at Sabie Bridge (now Skukuza). For transport he had donkeys and an ox-cart; his staff consisted of a few black helpers.

One of Stevenson-Hamilton's first tasks was to remove all the black squatters from the reserve, settling them closer to their traditional tribal chiefs in adjacent areas. By a process of attrition these tribesmen had done more than their share in reducing animal numbers.

Realizing the enormity of his task, Stevenson-Hamilton approached the Native Affairs Department, which at that time was responsible for the reserve, and was authorised to employ two white assistants – each at a salary of £1 a day – and a small number of black police, who each received £2 a month. These rangers had to patrol the reserve, to combat poaching and make themselves thoroughly disagreeable to anyone wishing to molest the animals.

The land reaching north from the Sabie river to the Olifants river was home to an even richer conglomeration of animal life than the Sabie Game Reserve, and Stevenson-Hamilton dearly wanted this area to be conserved. Although divided into numerous large farms during the previous century, and owned by the State as well as various land companies and wealthy individuals, the land had not been worked because of its wildness and the fear of malaria. By negotiating with the government and the landowners, Stevenson-Hamilton even-

The Stevenson-Hamilton Memorial Library in Skukuza is well worth a visit.

tually secured agreements which guaranteed the protection of the animal and plant-life in the area. These agreements, which had to be renewed every five years, were Gazetted for the first time in 1902.

In 1903 the Shingwedzi Game Reserve was proclaimed, Stevenson-Hamilton and his team becoming responsible for this area as well. The new reserve covered the entire area between the Limpopo and Letaba rivers, which gave Stevenson-Hamilton control over nearly 37 000 square kilometres.

But lack of real authority severely hampered efforts to curtail poaching. Those poachers who were caught had to be marched all the way to the regional magistrate at Barberton or Lydenburg. This ridiculous situation was remedied when the Legislative Council appointed Stevenson-Hamilton as a Special Justice of the Peace, and gave powers of arrest and detention both to him and to his ranger staff. The great step forward brought a new dimension to the ability of these few men to effectively ensure the well-being of the wildlife in their care. Eventually Stevenson-Hamilton was appointed Native Commissioner and a customs official, so further extending his control.

Within a few short months of Stevenson-Hamilton's arrival in the reserve, he showed his outstanding qualities – drive, great physical energy, deep insight and a valuable ability to converse and negotiate with politicians.

But his greatest test still lay ahead, for resentment against Stevenson-Hamilton and his staff of rangers steadily grew. He had made it clear that he would not tolerate any shooting of game, and set an example by living on army rations. His initial warnings were disregarded, but when finally he successfully prosecuted two senior police officers for poaching, shooting of animals decreased – though the hostility of the people on neighbouring land increased.

Lush summer growth carpets a hill near Mooiplaas.

Viewed in its historical setting, that resentment is perhaps easier to understand. Those living in the Lowveld were hard people, living under hard conditions; they were practical people accustomed to wresting a livelihood from their environment. They lived for the present, not for the future. Stevenson-Hamilton was one of the pitifully few with the foresight to know that what he was fighting for would surely be appreciated some distant day.

As increasing numbers of people settled in the adjoining areas, the farming potential of the Sabie Game Reserve posed a serious threat to its existence. Questions were being flung at Stevenson-Hamilton and officialdom. What exactly was the benefit of the reserve? The animals were regarded as wild and dangerous, useful only when dead as meat and hides. The bushveld itself was held to harbour diseases and, in general, was regarded as a hindrance to the advance of civilization.

Stevenson-Hamilton and the Sabie Game Reserve now entered the most critical stage in their fight for survival. In 1912 a five-year agreement with the land associations expired and these placed heavy pressure on the Administrator of the Transvaal. Stevenson-Hamilton could only battle to keep encroachment into the reserve as minimal as possible. Eventually sheep-farmers were allowed to let their stock into certain parts – including the present Pretoriuskop area – for grazing during winter. The land between the Sabie and Olifants rivers was also thrown open to winter grazing. However, Stevenson-Hamilton retained the power to prevent shooting of animals and enforced this rule rigidly. This, combined with the fee the farmers paid for grazing and their losses to lions, had the farmers up in arms.

Commissions of enquiry investigated the concept and feasibility of game reserves. Stevenson-Hamilton rallied, and rose to the occasion. As early as 1905 he had foreseen that reserves would need a reason for existence, and one acceptable to the general public. So he planted the idea of a 'National Park' where visitors could view the animals and scenery for relaxation and enjoyment. At first the public was unreceptive, but as the 20th century advanced people's attitudes and general way of life were changing. The Transvaal Game Protection Association advanced the same idea of a 'National Park', and several public figures now rose to encourage game conservation.

A railway line, which ran through the Sabie Game Reserve, had been opened to link the farming areas south of the reserve with those in the north. To justify its existence, the railway authorities wanted the land adjoining the railway line to be opened for farming.

Stevenson-Hamilton was now at his lowest ebb, with an almost overwhelming array of forces lined against him. Resiliently he came up with ingenious plans to turn the reserve into a financial asset, including a scheme of rearing young animals for eventual sale to overseas zoos and institutions. In the event, he had no need to resort to this. The concept of national parks was beginning to gain support.

A commission of enquiry appointed in 1916 finally laid down recommendations in 1918 which included the following statement: '. . . we recommend that the policy of the Administration should be directed toward the creation of the area ultimately as a great national park where the natural and prehistoric conditions of our country can be preserved for all time.' It proposed that private land in the protected areas be exchanged for government land in adjoining areas, or that farmers be compensated for land which was appropriated. Again the farmers hedged, they did not accept the proposals.

In 1923 the South African Railways organized a series of fortnightly tours which included a number of tourist attractions in the Lowveld. Of necessity, the train had to pass through the Sabie Game Reserve. The stretch through the reserve was scheduled to take place at night, but Stevenson-Hamilton negotiated an arrangement that allowed tourists to stop briefly for a meal around a camp-fire. To the Railway authorities' absolute surprise, it appeared that the Sabie Game Reserve was the highlight of the tour. The public wanted to, and enjoyed watching animals in their natural environment.

With a change of government, Piet Grobler – a grand-nephew of President Paul Kruger and himself a keen conservationist and sympathizer of the 'National Park' concept – became the Minister of Lands. Stevenson-Hamilton ceaselessly persevered in speeding the movement which had now swung in his favour, and the transition of the Sabie Game Reserve to a national park seemed inevitable.

Finally, on May 31st, 1926, Piet Grobler proclaimed the Kruger National Park which was to include the old Sabie and Shingwedzi Game Reserves as well as the land between the two. Stevenson-Hamilton's 'Cinderella', as he called it, had become a princess.

Diminutive only in size, Stevenson-Hamilton had proved himself a man of considerable force and intellect. With a pathetically small staff of men he had struggled to suppress poaching, nurtured the devastated herds back to increase and abundance, and endured the bitter enmity of those opposed to conservation.

. . . and the development

Tourism and Technical Services. The proclamation of the Kruger National Park and simultaneous safe passage through Parliament of the National Parks Act, allowed Stevenson-Hamilton and his men effectively to plan for the future. No longer were the uncertainty and threats of exploitation by land associations or private individuals a brake on efforts to progress.

Their budget was still severely restricted, but in 1927 the staff began road-building and providing accommodation for tourists, and by the end of the year visitors could travel to Pretoriuskop and view animals along a circular road near the camp. The camp itself was merely a log enclosure within which visitors had to make do as best they could. Often the rangers would give up their own homes so that tourists could have a few more comforts.

But the first roads were built more to link the various section-rangers with headquarters at Skukuza than to provide good game drives for visitors. Camps were established near the homes of these rangers so that the staff could provide some control and protection. Building methods for both roads and camps were of necessity crude and primitive. Huts were made of local stone, logs, thatch and mud; large gangs would chop down trees and vegetation to clear a rough track. There were eight rangers, each with a small number of black assistants to do the work: build roads, build huts, keep a vigilant eye on the never-ending bands of poachers, and patrol a wilderness area larger than the state of Israel. Isolation and poor communication added to their load.

Despite the difficulties and lack of funds, the men persevered: by 1928, 122 miles of road had been completed, in 1930, 450 miles and by 1936, 900 miles of road were available. During summer these roads would be transformed into muddy quagmires in which cars would get hopelessly stuck; after a good storm, dry stream-beds would become raging torrents, washing away roads and blocking all traffic until the water subsided. And yet the people came; they loved it.

For crossings of the main rivers, Stevenson-Hamilton used discarded mining equipment – donated by a Mr Selby of the Wildlife Preservation Society – to construct pontoons which ferried each car over the Sabie and Crocodile rivers. For the shallow Sand river, just north of the Sabie, poles were cut, wired together, and laid across the river. 'It was an alarming method, until one got used to it, for the bridge swayed and sank to the shallow bottom of the stream, with passage of every car,' Stevenson-Hamilton recorded.

By the end of 1929 a pontoon was ready to ferry visitors across the Olifants river, and another milestone had been reached. While a concrete bridge over the Letaba was being built, the rangers at Punda

Nyamundwa dam which lies between Skukuza and Pretoriuskop, is a favoured drinking spot.

Maria and Shingwedzi worked feverishly to clear a road to the south. And so, before the middle of 1933, visitors could travel from Malelane in the extreme south, right up to the baobab-dotted hills of Pafuri in the distant north of the Park. It was a momentous day.

The stream of visitors kept increasing, forcing the already hard-pressed staff to increase their efforts. By 1930 six camps with about 100 concrete huts provided accommodation, but the demand for more never diminished. So fast had the popularity of the Park spread that from the meagre beginnings of three cars entering in 1927, yielding a total income of £3 for that year, the figure blossomed to 6 000 cars carrying 26 000 people in 1935. Stevenson-Hamilton's vision had become reality; his long years of efforts were being rewarded. The Park filled an unexpected need in the public, they crowded to get in.

As in any new venture of considerable size and scope, teething problems were inevitable. The Park remained open to visitors throughout the year, and though in the winter months all went well, when the summer rains fell the roads became muddy traps, cars were stranded, and malaria gripped people in its feverish hand.

In March 1929, two truckloads of American visitors entered at Crocodile Bridge on a drive to Lower Sabie. They drove into a thunderstorm which reduced the road to a slippery mass of treacherous mud. Turning around to return to Crocodile Bridge, they found their path now blocked by a stream, but decided to try getting through. The first truck went in and promptly overturned. Its drenched occupants took to the trees as lions started roaring in the vicinity. It was thus that a ranger found them a few hours later.

17

The now thoroughly disillusioned Americans, several of them suffering from malaria, returned home where their story appeared in the newspapers and labelled South Africa as a 'death trap'. Understandably, the decision was taken that from 1930 the Park should remain open to visitors only during the dry winter months, though the Pretoriuskop area remained open because its relatively high position rendered it free of malaria. Not for many years – until better roads and bridges guaranteed safe passage, and malaria control became more effective – did this ruling change.

Stevenson-Hamilton finally retired in April 1946 – after nearly 44 years of unmatched service to the nature reserve he dearly loved. His headquarters had already been given his Shangaan name – 'Skukuza', meaning 'the man who sweeps clean'. Later a magnificent memorial library bearing his name was to be built in the same camp. He died on December 10th, 1957, aged 90. When his wife Hilda died in 1979 their ashes were scattered on a hill covered with massive granite boulders a few kilometres south-west of Skukuza. Stevenson-Hamilton had chosen this site himself among the timeless rocks thrust high above the surrounding country that had become his special home.

Colonel J.A.B. Sandenbergh became the second warden, and the volume of tourists continued to grow. In 1948 there were nearly 59 000; in 1955 the number of visitors exceeded 100 000; in 1964 it rose to above 200 000; then to more than 300 000 in 1968; and in 1982 it reached 463 000.

The glow of a camp fire brings a sense of comfort to the night on one of the highly popular wilderness trails.

This increasing flood of visitors made it necessary to again revise some of the management policies. To ensure a standard and more appropriate service to tourists, in 1955 the National Parks Board took control of all trading and restaurant facilities from the private concerns which had previously operated in the various camps. Since then profits from these activities have been channelled back into the Park and used to benefit its wildlife.

Roads suffered from the heavy and increasing tourist traffic. Simple paths cleared of trees and stones were no longer acceptable, for under such heavy wear they became deeply rutted and eroded, choked in thick layers of powdery dust. However, an internal roads department, established in 1950, soon matured to provide better roads with longer lasting surfaces. No longer were the roads washed away after every heavy downpour; vehicles were not as likely to get bogged down; and bridges were being built to span rivers and streams which had previously blocked traffic. At the same time, the old combat against malaria-carrying mosquitoes was gaining momentum, using new pesticides discovered during World War II, and new drugs highly effective in preventing malaria also became readily available. All this combined to make the Park less of a threat to human life in summer. The Lowveld was being tamed.

It was now safe to again open the Park to visitors throughout the year – a process carried out in gradual stages: Skukuza remained open as of 1962; in 1963 visitors could travel at any time of the year up to the Tshokwane picnic-site; in 1964 this was extended to include the whole area south of the Letaba river; and, finally, in the 1970's the entire Park was opened to visitors all year round.

But again new problems arose. Better roads and less malaria attracted more visitors, again increasing the traffic load. After much heated debate and argument, in the early 1960's it was decided to tar all arterial roads linking the larger camps. In 1965 the first, from Skukuza to Numbi entrance gate near Pretoriuskop, was completed. Other roads slowly appeared, radiating in all directions until finally even Pafuri far in the north boasted a tarred link snaking across the silent mopane-covered hills. By 1982, 742 kilometres of tarred road and 1 200 kilometres of gravel road were open for game-viewing.

On February 1st, 1969, yet another milestone was reached when Commercial Airways (Comair) flew in the first batch of tourists to land at the Skukuza Airport. In years to come this would prove a highly popular service catering to the needs of many.

The old Selati railway line, so filled with poignant history, finally fell to the needs of practical considerations. When Stevenson-Hamilton arrived in 1902, the line extended only as far as the present Skukuza, abruptly ending on the southern bank of the Sabie river. But when the line was completed in 1912 it reached Zoekmekaar, and in the ensuing decades the raucous whistles of thundering steam engines shattered the bushveld quiet; often animals were killed as the metal monsters roared their relentless way through the surrounding bush.

19

Finally, in 1973, the trains came to a permanent halt and the lines were pulled up. The magnificently photogenic bridge across the Sabie river, in plain view from much of Skukuza camp, remains a silent memorial to those rowdy and opportunistic days of the early 20th century.

Today the Kruger Park is alive and well. A staff of 2 954 – 1 280 of these resident at Skukuza – looks after the well-being of both wildlife and visitors. Tourist numbers continue to increase and the clamour for more accommodation keeps rising accordingly.

The wilderness trails, which were introduced in 1979 for the more adventurous visitors, are now so popular that they are fully reserved a year in advance. A new hiking trail is planned for the near future, and several more camps with luxury accommodation will be built during the next ten years.

But what then? Our population growth is such that even with these new camps there will still be a demand for more. The Park is rapidly approaching the level where it can take no more visitors without intruding on the concept that this is a wilderness area, to be preserved as a wilderness area, and to be conserved for the benefit of the wildlife in it. How far does one go without upsetting the balance between man's interests and the interests of wildlife? Let us not forget that this Park exists for the benefit of the animals and plants, in as undisturbed a state as possible.

Wildlife Management and Research. When the old Sabie Game Reserve was proclaimed in 1898, all that it contained were the scattered remnants of large animal herds which had once roamed this bushveld Eden. For nearly half a century they had been harassed and slaughtered by increasing numbers of white hunters armed with rifles, and the diminishing herds were further eroded by the snares, traps and spears of tribesmen living in the area. Then, almost as a spiteful afterthought, Nature dealt a calamitous and near-disastrous blow. A massive outbreak of rinderpest swept through the Lowveld in 1896, leaving in its wake untold thousands of bloated corpses. Except for a few stragglers, the entire buffalo population had been wiped out. With this epidemic too, and for reasons unknown, the hated tsetse fly disappeared into the depths of Portuguese East Africa.

Stevenson-Hamilton arrived in 1902 to find the reserve severely depleted of animals. To help the herds of antelope regain a foothold and struggle along the road to abundance, he declared war on all predatory mammals. Lions, leopards, cheetahs, wild-dogs, even reptiles and predatory birds did not escape the bullets of the warden and his staff. Slowly, but noticeably, the herds of herbivores began increasing, until they had a better chance of survival. This was the beginning of a policy of wildlife management designed to ensure the continuation of all animal and plant species within the reserve. Man had originally stepped in to decimate the animal herds; now it was up to man to restore that balance which had existed prior to his arrival.

Researchers prepare immobilizing drugs to capture cheetah.

The more one learns about James Stevenson-Hamilton, the more convinced one becomes that this was an exceptional man. Besides a deep interest in wildlife, he had no qualifications for his job of game management and conservation. Yet his every action created unique precedents – most of which are still followed today.

In 1905 he visited Inhambane, in Portuguese East Africa, to obtain eland which he hoped would serve as a breeding herd to re-establish the now non-existent herds of the Sabie and Shingwedzi reserves. He returned with a young bull and a female calf, which were kept in a pen at Sabie Bridge (Skukuza) where they eventually increased to a herd of ten. But while Stevenson-Hamilton was on active service in Europe during World War I, all aspects of conservation, management and administration in the reserve declined, the herd of eland was also neglected and all died. The first attempt at re-establishing a disappeared species had failed.

Stevenson-Hamilton appears to have had a three-pronged strategy to ensure the survival of the wildlife in his care. Firstly, an unremitting battle to apprehend poachers and reduce poaching. Secondly, a roughly monitored programme to reduce the number of carnivores, particularly lions, so that herbivores could regain some semblance of their previous abundance. But his third task, self-imposed, was his greatest. This was a long drawn-out political struggle to keep the unspoilt wilderness from the hungry clutches of the farming and mining companies – and it brought to light his tenacity, ingenuity and formidable debating powers. The period 1910 to 1923 nearly saw the downfall of the Sabie Game Reserve, and it is extremely unlikely that the Kruger National Park of today would exist but for his efforts.

In 1896 the rinderpest epidemic almost exterminated the African buffalo. Today there are more than 25 000 in the Park.

Though the proclamation of the Kruger National Park led to a slight easing of financial pressures, resources were still limited, and it was only when money became more readily available that Stevenson-Hamilton could add a fourth dimension to his management strategy: to spread and stabilize over wider areas the supply of water available to the animals. During the dry winter they had always congested around a few permanent waterholes and along the major rivers, which often led to severe over-grazing and trampling of the nearby veld. If he could supply watering-points in other areas, the animals would become spread more evenly and the veld would suffer less.

A novel idea, and intended for a large area, this would involve substantial sums of money to which Stevenson-Hamilton had no ordinary access. Again he spread the word, ably presented the benefit of his scheme, and people became convinced of the logic of his concept. Friends organized fund-raising campaigns, and as money dribbled in Stevenson-Hamilton could make a start. He began sinking boreholes at Pretoriuskop in 1933, and by 1935 14 successful holes had been sunk at various strategic sites, where windmills spread-eagled the holes to pump out the life-giving water. Since that time the water-for-game programme has continued and new dams or windmills go up every year.

The constant protection given to the animals allowed the populations of the various species to multiply at an ever-increasing rate, with competition for food and space becoming more and more evident. It also became clear that scientific research was necessary to study the requirements of key species which determined or influenced the survival of other species. Such knowledge could be used for better management of each species and for the ultimate benefit of all the animals and plants.

In 1950 a scientific research section was established and the appointment of Dr T.G. Nel in October that year heralded a new era, one which would lead to a vastly improved and reliable wildlife management policy. Headquarters for this section was established at Skukuza, and in 1951 another biologist was appointed.

One of the research section's first tasks was to devise and implement an effective burning programme. The Park was divided into a series of 400 blocks, each separated by firebreak roads to prevent fire from causing such extensive damage as it had previously. Smaller experimental blocks were established in the various habitat types to monitor on a long-term basis the effect of the various burning regimes. This data has resulted in an effective strategy of burning for the greater area of the Park.

A seemingly simple move, which would eventually have far-reaching effects, was initiated in 1959. The Kruger National Park had as natural boundaries the Crocodile river in the south and the Luvuvhu river in the north. To the east stood the Lebombo mountains, but innumerable passes and valleys allowed the free passage of animals. The western boundary ran through an open plain, with no natural barrier to the animals. During the winter large herds of wildebeest and zebra would migrate from the parched plains to the moist foothills of the Drakensberg in the west, blissfully unaware of the arbitrary line officialdom had designated as the western boundary. Thus animals and poachers alike could move with relative ease across both western and eastern boundaries.

This free movement of game – especially along the western side – presented problems, not only because of the large number of animals being shot on the adjoining farms, but because of increasing insistence by veterinary departments that the wild animals posed a threat to domestic stock by spreading foot-and-mouth disease. In 1959, therefore, work was started to fence the entire western boundary and in 1975 the international border forming the eastern side was also fenced with elephant-resistant cable.

The fencing of the boundaries created an artificial system. Although very large, the Kruger National Park was not a natural ecological unit and the traditional winter migration paths were now excluded by the fences. With the animals restricted to a confined area, water had to be supplied, and controlled burning of vegetation exercised to ensure sufficient grazing.

Under such conditions – and with the added factor of indiscriminate protection of all animal species – imbalances were almost certain to occur. And they did. The phenomenal increase in the elephant population exemplifies this. From having been reduced in the Lowveld to a mere handful of survivors around the turn of the century, elephant numbers slowly recovered and increased within the protection of the reserves. In 1946 Colonel Sandenbergh estimated the number of ele-

Drugged rhino receiving antidote after removal from quarantine area.

phants in the entire Kruger Park at between 400 and 500. Using a light aircraft, the first aerial count of the larger mammals in 1959 showed the elephant population had doubled to 986. In the same year fencing began, and elephants could no longer filter off into less dense areas when their population levels became too high. During another aerial count in 1964 it was found that the elephant population had exploded to 2 374. The buffalo population had shown a similar trend.

The incredible rise in numbers of these two species was alarming. The damage they caused to vegetation was becoming increasingly apparent and would eventually threaten their own existence as well as that of other species. After lengthy study and computer analysis, it was eventually decided on November 30th, 1965 that where a species became a threat to itself, other animals and the vegetation, the population should be reduced to a level which could be adequately supported by the environment. From 1966, therefore, controlled culling, especially of buffalo and elephant populations, was introduced.

When this practice became public knowledge a veritable hornet's nest was stirred. Thousands of words were written in newspapers and magazines regarding the so-called 'slaughter', raising a spectre of blood-thirsty officials decimating vast herds of elephant and buffalo with little concern for their suffering. Nothing could be further from the truth. Only now, nearly 20 years later, has the public begun to accept that control of animal populations is, in fact, necessary and humane.

By taking into account factors such as the impact of buffalo and elephant on vegetation, and the needs of other species living in close association with the buffalo and elephant in their preferred areas, it was decided to stabilize the elephant population at between 7 000 and 7 500, and the buffalo population at 25 000.

Another programme which aroused considerable interest among visitors was the drug-darting of animals for re-location or scientific study. An adapted cross-bow fitted with a special dart filled with an anaesthetising drug, could be used to temporarily sedate any animal long enough for it to be caged for transportation to other areas or parks, for the treatment of snare-wounds, to be marked with ear-tags and neckbands and released, or merely to obtain blood-samples and measurements. In this way hippopotamuses were drugged and transferred from Kruger Park to the Addo Elephant Park, rhino were re-established in the Kruger Park from other areas such as Zululand, and elephant and lion were marked for a study of their migratory patterns.

As well as such team efforts, many excellent and authoritative studies have been made by individual zoologists on the ecology of various animal species such as impala, zebra, lion, elephant, roan antelope and others. In the botanical field there have been several studies on the flora, including a long-term study on the trees of the Park by Piet van Wyk, present chief of research and information, which resulted in a monumental and lavishly illustrated, two-volume reference work for scientists and laymen.

Extensive veterinary research includes projects on the parasites and diseases of mammals, and a major study on the epidemiology of anthrax. This bacterial disease is prevalent in the northern areas of the Park and occasional epidemics occur, especially during unusually dry seasons. The very rare roan antelope are particularly susceptible to the disease, and anthrax kills large numbers of these and other animals. During the early 1970's the veterinarian and present assistant chief of research and information, Dr V. de Vos, devised an immunization programme which entails annual darting, from a helicopter, each roan antelope with an immunizing drug. A few massive outbreaks of this disease have resulted in the death of hundreds of the Park's animals in recent years.

At present ten scientific researchers and technical assistants stationed at Skukuza carry out field work throughout the Park. And though often they have come under critical fire, the continued survival and peaceful co-existence of all the animals and plants in this artificially created ecosystem is largely due to their genuine concern and efforts.

Colonel Sandenbergh, who took over the reins of control from Stevenson-Hamilton, was succeeded by Mr L.B. Steyn (1954-1961), Mr A.M. Brynard (1961-1970) who is now director of all national parks, and finally Dr U. de V. Pienaar, the pioneering biologist who since the 1950's has expertly nurtured and guided the scientific research division to its present status as one of the world leaders in the practice of conservation and management of wildlife.

In retrospect

Forged from the early years of turmoil and struggle when its very existence was precariously sustained by the sheer tenacity of a handful of people, the Kruger National Park today stands as a viable and flourishing monument to their memory – people like Paul Kruger and James Stevenson-Hamilton. They had the insight, they had the force of conviction, and they had the persistence not only to implement, but to maintain unwaveringly their belief and subsequent efforts to place an area of wilderness under legal protection as inviolate heritage for future generations. What sets them apart is that in an era where the untamed bushveld was regarded as land to be forcibly entered and recklessly plundered, they had the foresight to know that in times to come even remnants of these areas would be cherished for education and relaxation.

And so it is today. Kruger Park remains one of the few places on our earth where we can look back in the mirror at our past. Here nature re-enacts its daily life just as it did 200 or even 2 000 years ago. Though situated in and administered by South Africa, in essence it belongs to all people in all countries, for conservation should know no national boundaries, and benefits accrue not only to one country. So rapidly and vastly are we exploiting and modifying our earth today, that it is only to these small islands of artificially maintained natural wilderness that we can turn to remind us of our origins. More important, infinitely more important, it is only to these areas that we can refer to research the interdependencies and inter-relationships of organisms with which we share our earth, to see which essential links in this intricate web of life we dare not sever lest we cause our own downfall. Nature has existed over many millions of years, but man's present technology enables him to disrupt and modify that stable environment in moments. We are hurtling ahead with that process at an astounding rate. Only by having available these wildlife areas – to use correctly as little dictionaries or reference books – may we avoid making a tragic series of miscalculations in Man's future history.

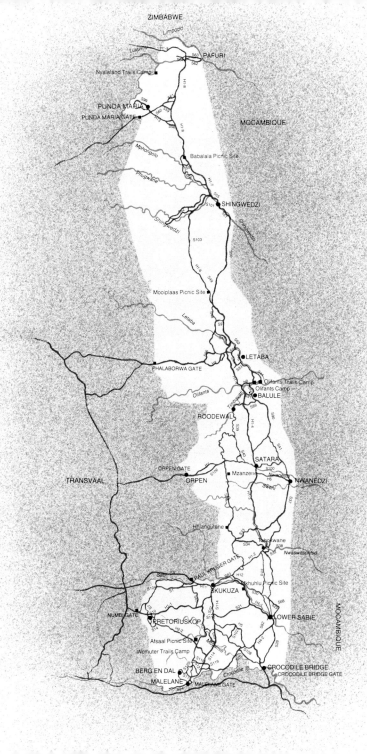

Topography

The Park lies in the north-eastern corner of the Republic of South Africa. More than 350 kilometres long and about 90 kilometres at its widest, it covers more than 19 000 square kilometres. Foreign countries abut three of the Park's boundaries: to the north lies Zimbabwe, Moçambique hugs the entire eastern perimeter, and the Republic of Venda nestles along the north-western border.

As an ecological unit, it is fortunate that natural barriers coincide with three boundaries – the Luvuvhu and Limpopo rivers in the north, the Crocodile river to the south, and the Lebombo mountain range along the east. Unfortunately, the western boundary is an arbitrary line cutting directly across traditional migration paths of large herds of antelope such as zebra and wildebeest. When, between 1959 and 1961, this boundary was fenced to prevent the spread of foot-and-mouth disease, these herds could no longer make their annual winter treks to the foothills of the Drakensberg for water and grazing. However, several hundred windmills and artificial waterholes have since been established to provide water for those animals which in times past trudged across the plains to quench their thirst.

Several major rivers such as the Crocodile, Sabie, Sand, Olifants, Letaba, Shingwedzi, Luvuvhu and Limpopo are spaced more or less evenly over the considerable length of the Park. These life-giving sources of water all flow from west to east, indicating a general slope of the land in that direction.

Height above sea-level varies from about 260 metres on the central grass-filled plains to 839 metres in the south-west near Malelane. As well as the Lebombo mountains thrusting up along the eastern edge of the Park, large hills are also found around Malelane and Pretoriuskop. Further north, towards Olifants camp and Letaba, occasional hills again appear, and hilly outcrops also occur around Punda Maria and at Pafuri. Elsewhere the Park tends to be rather flat, with gentle undulations and sporadic boulder-strewn granitic extrusions.

Climate. Daytime temperatures are rather high during summer, frequently reaching well over 40 °C but on average being about 30 °C. The nights are warm and tend to have minimum temperatures hovering around 18 °C.

During winter the days are usually cloudless and warm, with an average maximum temperature of 23 °C. It cools down rapidly in the late afternoon and the nights are cold, generally about 8 °C during the early hours before sunrise. Extreme minimum temperatures may be as low as -4 °C but these are very much the exception. The warmest months are December and January whilst the coolest weather is experienced in June and July.

Grass-filled plains of the northern Kruger Park.

Because it lies in the summer-rainfall region, the rainy season normally commences in September or October. December, January and February usually receive the heaviest downpours, after which the rainfall tapers off to little or no rain during June, July and August.

By monitoring the monthly rainfall in the various parts of the Park over a long period – in the case of Skukuza for more than 60 years – an interesting pattern has emerged. Definite wet and dry cycles, each lasting from eight to 12 years, alternate with each other and result in periods of extreme drought or devastating floods. If the same pattern continues, and there is no reason why it should not, a dry cycle can be expected for the greater part of the 1980's.

Except for the fairly high areas around Punda Maria, rainfall tends to be lowest in the northern parts of the Park and highest in the south. Thus Pafuri receives only an average 438 millimetres of rain each year, whereas Pretoriuskop has 744 millimetres.

These rainfall patterns are important to visitors seeking the best game-viewing. To see game, the best time is around June, July and August when all the smaller pools and streams have dried up and the animals concentrate around the larger dams and rivers. Most of these are situated close to tourist roads and, as many trees have dropped their leaves and the vegetation cover as a whole is reduced, it is much easier to locate and observe the animals.

Personally, I find this approach rather ill-considered as winter visitors miss the tremendous scenery of summer. A wide range of animals in sufficient numbers will still be seen, and luxuriant groves of trees in full bloom complement the rich green fields of revitalized grasses. Most of the larger mammals bear their young during this time when environmental conditions are most favourable. Flocks of bright and beautiful birds migrate in for the warm summer months when food and water abound, and all the animals appear healthy and content. The atmosphere for enjoying the wildlife and absorbing the character of the bushveld is so much better during summer.

29

Vegetation zones

The size of the Park, and particularly its north-south length, makes inevitable a considerable range of vegetation zones. Collectively these may be termed bushveld, but a number of distinct zones can be recognised within this 'overall' term.

The drier northern area, stretching from the Olifants river through to the Limpopo, is predominantly mopane *(Colophospermum mopane)* country. The western half of this section consists of fairly tall mopane trees mixed with stands of the equally tough red bush-willow *(Combretum apiculatum)*. East of this through to the Lebombo mountains are vast unbroken stretches covered by short, stunted mopane trees of uniform height with few other trees to break the monotony. Further north, towards Punda Maria, the soil and rainfall changes, encouraging luxuriant stands of mopane forest. And towards Pafuri and the Limpopo the majestic baobab trees *(Adansonia digitata)* become increasingly abundant, towering as ageless sentinels over the surrounding vegetation.

Mixed woodland typifies the area around Skukuza.

South of the Olifants river the vegetation diversifies. Large, grassy plains with abundantly scattered knobthorn *(Acacia nigrescens)*, marula *(Sclerocarya caffra)* and leadwood trees *(Combretum imberbe)* dominate the landscape around Satara and in the eastern strip running more or less from the Olifants river and covering the camp-sites at Nwanedzi, Lower Sabie and Crocodile Bridge.

The south-western part of the Park, including Skukuza and a wide strip along the western boundary up to Orpen Gate, consists mainly of thorny thickets and fairly dense stands of red bush-willow, knobthorn, tamboti *(Spirostachys africana)*, marula, and a wide variety of other species.

A fairly small but distinct zone is formed in the high-lying areas around Pretoriuskop where silver terminalia *(Terminalia sericea)* and shrubby sicklebush *(Dichrostachys cinerea)* are dominant. Stands of tall grass separate the trees, which also include the familiar marula and a range of acacias.

Heavily wooded forests adjoin all the major rivers, with magnificent trees such as the sycamore fig *(Ficus sycomorus)*, Natal mahogany *(Trichilia emetica)*, fever trees *(Acacia xanthophloea)*, and nyala trees *(Xanthocercis zambesiaca)* among the largest and most beautiful.

Lush riverine growth adjoins the Luvuvhu river.

31

Trees to be seen in Kruger Park

The Park provides habitats for a range of more than 300 different species of tree. The baobab and sausage tree are among these which attract attention because of their unusual appearance; others, including the tree fuchsia and sycamore fig, have magnificent stature and some are just downright beautiful (long-tail cassia, coral tree, wisteria and others). Their interest aroused by trees such as these, visitors often start looking at the less spectacular species – and find that they, too, have a beauty and elegance all of their own, for all trees are fascinating when afforded a closer look.

Some of the best-loved of the Park's trees are:

Apple Leaf, also known as **Rain Tree** *(Lonchocarpus capassa)*. Notable for its awkward and rather formless appearance rather than natural beauty, this tree is found throughout the Park. It grows to a height of about 18 metres but lacks the compact, rounded and pleasing habit of most other large trees. Instead, the rain tree thrusts skywards a bare stem which somehow seems to lose direction along the way, then throws out a few twisted branches which seem equally incapable of finding aim. As though hiding its shame, each branch has, near its end, a spreading crown of broad, greyish-green leaves which afford it some little beauty. Contrary to this slightly harsh appraisal, a few specimens actually attain an appealing and very pleasing shape.

Its common name probably derives from the unusual habit of a group of insects which frequent these trees in summer. Belonging to the family *Cercopidae,* and generally known as spittle-bugs, the nymphs or larvae of these insects produce a froth by bubbling air through juices sucked out from the tree. The frothy liquid covers the insects, providing them with protection from the drying effect of the sun and against most insect predators. Such a large quantity of this frothy liquid is present at times that the excess drips off as 'rain'.

During October and November, the tree produces rounded bunches of small mauve-coloured flowers. The seeds which follow are borne in pods similar to those found on acacias.

Perhaps because of the very appearance of the tree, there is a quaint tribal belief that the immediate family of a person who chops down such a tree will wander from home, never to return.

Baobab *(Adansonia digitata)*. This species surely needs no introduction to anyone with even a passing interest in wildlife. Its extreme girth and dominating appearance must make it one of the most widely known – and most frequently photographed – trees in the world.

Although scattered specimens occur as far south as near Tshokwane, baobabs are common only in the Pafuri area. Here many gigantic specimens can be seen dotting the mopane landscape.

Apple leaf, *Lonchocarpus capassa*.

The trees generally reach a height of about 25 metres and may have a stem diameter of 10 metres. (One particularly large tree, outside the Park near Duiwelskloof, has a reputed girth of 46,8 metres, indeed a monstrous specimen!) The thick stem ends rather abruptly, then sends out a random series of short branches with tapering ends. This truncated habit gives the tree an obese appearance, which nevertheless is overshadowed by a feeling of fascination which large specimens evoke.

The baobab's bark is usually greyish, but sometimes reddish-brown. The stem is gnarled and flabby, much like molten wax running down the side of a candle.

During summer the trees are normally well covered with glossy, bright green leaves which have paler undersides. The foliage falls with winter's approach, giving the tree a stark and forlorn appearance, like a survivor from a previous age who, doomed to a timeless existence, now stands in grim acceptance. The trees grow to a very ripe old age, and it has been estimated that ages of about 4 000 years for trees with a 10-metre girth would not be unusual.

Despite their almost timeless and somewhat invulnerable appearance, baobabs have a very soft wood which rapidly disintegrates when the tree dies. It literally crumbles into a mass of disorganized fibres which may occasionally be seen along the road in the Pafuri area.

Baobab *(Adansonia digitata)* in the Pafuri area.

Large white flowers droop down from near the end of branchlets. Usually borne in November, the blooms generally do not last very long before turning brown and being shed. The rather large and attractive fruit grows to about the size of a big fist and is roughly oval to tear-drop in shape. It is covered with a dense layer of fine velvety fur. Baboons eat the fruit for the pulp and seeds inside.

The trunks of many of the trees in the northern area have been badly scarred by elephants which scrape off the bark to eat. Baboons and elephants seem to be the only animals consistently feeding from baobabs.

Tribesmen use its products in a variety of ways. P. van Wyk, in his two-volume work, *Trees of the Kruger National Park,* mentions that malaria and dysentery are treated by using derivatives of the bark and fruit. The fruit is also used to make a refreshing drink, or pulped as a soup ingredient. Porridge is apparently also made from parts of the root.

Tribal legend – unkind to both the baobab and that much maligned beast the hyena – has it that at the beginning of things, the gods provided all the animals with seeds and plants to cultivate. Last of all came the hyena and it duly received the baobab. In keeping with its supposedly stupid nature, the hyena planted the tree upside down. During winter, when the branches are bare, the tree indeed looks as though it has been uprooted and replanted wrong end up.

The Euphorbias *(Euphorbia* spp.). Most visitors think of these plants as cacti, but in fact they belong to the same family as the common garden poinsettia and trees from which manioc and tapioca are produced. Four members of the genus *Euphorbia* commonly occur in the Park and reach tree-size. Like forgotten relics from some prehistoric age, they push up their succulent frames on hills, rocky outcrops and in the Lebombo mountains in the east. Occasional specimens also occur on the open plains. The trees grow about eight metres high – though some reach as much as 15 metres – and prefer well-drained soils.

The yellow flowers are small and attract large numbers of insects which can be easily photographed whilst contentedly sipping the nectar. The fruits are divided into three compartments and become pink, red or purple when mature.

A well-known feature of *Euphorbia* trees is the poisonous nature of the milky latex which they exude when they are cut or otherwise damaged. Children especially should be kept away from these trees as painful blisters develop where the latex comes into contact with the skin, whilst blindness – or at least excruciating pain – will result if any of the 'milk' gets into the eyes.

The toxicity of some of these trees is clearly illustrated by the fact that tribesmen throw mutilated *Euphorbia* branches into pools, causing fish to float to the top, poisoned into insensibility. All that remains is to scoop the fish from the water.

Top left: Double-tiered euphorbia on the way to Nwanedzi. Top right: Rock wild figs *(Ficus soldanella)* flourish on stony hills. Above: Sycamore figs *(Ficus sycomorus)* abound on river-bank slopes.

Rock Wild Fig *(Ficus soldanella)*. One of the more striking and unusual trees, the rock wild fig is fairly common and, strangely, tends to grow on rocky hills among boulders where little or no soil is found. Rearing skyward from the bare rock, it seems to flourish in the midst of a barren earth. The tree is small when compared with other fig trees, reaching a height of only six metres when full-grown. The attractive creamy-white stem contrasts well with the broad dark green leaves. The tree is supported by a mass of roots, draped over the rocky base and cemented into any cracks or crevices.

The fruits of the rock wild fig dangle from the leaf-axils singly or in pairs. Baboons, monkeys and birds have a great liking for them, as do warthogs and a wide range of antelope which feed on fallen fruits.

Sycamore Fig *(Ficus sycomorus)*. Commonly found along the banks of all the major rivers and streams, the sycamore fig is one of the giants, easily reaching a height of about 20 metres and forming one of the most luxuriant and beautiful of all African trees. When full-grown, the stem is thick, covered in a paper-thin yellowish bark which readily flakes off to expose the bright green living bark below. The stem soon splits into a radiating series of graciously flowing branches below a rounded canopy of fairly rough-textured green leaves. Thick clusters of soft, fur-covered figs dot the uppermost branches for the greater part of the year. These fruits are avidly eaten by baboons, monkeys, birds, fruit bats and, when they have dropped to the ground, by a wide range of mammals as well.

Like those of all fig trees, the flowers of this species are enclosed within the fruit and have to be pollinated by very small wasps which tunnel their way into and out of the fig. As is often the case, there is only one species of wasp responsible for pollinating the sycamore fig. Female wasps collect pollen grains and store them in special pouches on the body. When they enter another fig these pollen grains are deposited on the female flowers. In this way an absolutely essential partnership has evolved between the tree and the wasp – the tree providing food for the wasp, and the wasp ensuring pollination for the tree.

Jackal Berry *(Diospyros mespiliformis)*. Moderately common but never really plentiful, this species has a definite preference for the banks of rivers and streams, where it often reaches a height of 20 metres and makes a fairly attractive tree. The largest and best specimens occur along the Luvuvhu river at Pafuri where they may sometimes be confused with nyala trees. Except for a short period in mid-spring when the leaves are shed, the tree is generally well covered to form a rounded, but somewhat ragged crown.

The trunk is generally some two metres in diameter, and has blackish-grey bark which is cracked and broken up into small rows of roughly square blocks. The elongate leaves are tough, with glossy yellowy-green to dark green upper surfaces and matt green undersides.

As with the marula, male and female flowers are borne on different trees. Both sexes are a creamy-white and resemble miniature, elongate vases. The flower clusters huddle between the leaves, and are generally most plentiful in December and January. The fruits are shiny green, rounded berries.

Inside each fruit are two to six bean-shaped, dark brown seeds, hard and covered in a jelly-like substance. When ripe, the fruits turn yellowy-brown and are apparently very tasty, for tribesmen preserve and make an alcoholic beverage from them. Various parts of the tree are used to treat ailments such as dysentery, ringworm, even leprosy. Skin sores, wounds and persistent coughs can also be treated. Although the fruit is eagerly eaten by a wide range of birds and animals, few animals appear to browse the leaves. Jackals often feed on the fallen berries, hence the tree's common name.

Leadwood *(Combretum imberbe)*. Scattered throughout the Park, but more common near streams and rivers, leadwood is abundant in the southern half, especially near the Moçambique border.

The tree normally grows about 20 metres high with a single fairly thick trunk which divides into a series of branches to form a rounded crown. Although attractive, the tree never really develops a thick canopy of leaves.

The characteristic ash-grey bark is split into neatly patterned, elongate blocks. The grey-green oblong leaflets are very tough. During November and December, numerous small yellowy-green flowers are borne in clusters arranged along thin twigs sprouting from the joints of the leaflets as well as along small branches. Though smaller and yellow, the fruits are similar to those of the closely allied red bush-willow, having four 'keels' or 'wings'.

As its common name implies, the wood is very hard, heavy, and known to campers as excellent for making fires. As in the case of red bush-willow, fires made from this wood give coals which give off great heat and last a very long time. The ashes are used as whitewash for painting walls of kraal huts.

Long-tail Cassia *(Cassia abbreviata* subsp. *beareana)*. This small tree, generally about five metres high, has a distinct ornamental appearance when in full bloom or garbed in summer foliage, and seems somewhat out of place between the surrounding drab acacias or other associated trees. It is fairly common south of the Olifants river, but also occurs in scattered localities up to the Limpopo.

The long-tail cassia is best known for its brilliant yellow flowers which blanket the tree in August and September. In full bloom, the trees form such an attractive sight that few people can resist stopping for a closer look.

The pods are also distinctive. Very long and very slender, they resemble lengths of thin sausage hung out for drying. The term 'long-tail' is undoubtedly derived from these blackish pods which are some-

The jackal berry *(Diospyros mespiliformis)* (top left) towers above its bushveld counterparts.
Top right: Leadwood *(Combretum imberbe)*. Above: Long-tail cassia *(Cassia abbreviata)*
in midday heat near Tshokwane.

times nearly a metre in length. Numerous flattened seeds are released when the pods split open whilst still on the tree.

Like most other Park trees, a medicinal use has been found for this species. Blackwater fever and malaria are treated with extracts from its roots, and, especially in the case of blackwater fever, this treatment seems to be effective. The bark is also powdered for use on abscesses.

Marula *(Sclerocarya caffra)*. This common tree is well known to many South Africans for the intoxicating effect of its over-ripe fruit when brewed, or distilled into a brandy. In the Park it is one of the most widespread of all tree species, being fairly common everywhere, but especially abundant south of the Olifants river. Generally growing to 15 or 18 metres, it is well formed, with a thick straight stem branching well above the ground to form a broadly round canopy. The stem is grey but rounded discs of bark continually peel away to expose pale bark below. This gives the stem an attractively blotched appearance.

In summer the trees are densely clothed with shiny green to greygreen leaves. Inconspicuous small flowers usually appear in August and September. Initially these are red, but whiten when they open. Male and female flowers are borne on separate trees, ensuring the cross-fertilization which provides genetic diversity – so giving, to some individuals at least, sufficient leeway to adapt when environmental conditions change. Genetic diversity is therefore, in a sense, the backbone of evolution, making the continued existence of a particular species of plant or animal more likely.

Its green, oval fruits are probably the marula's best-known feature. About the size of a wild fig, they are dropped in large numbers during January and February, turning yellow on the ground as they ripen.The smooth thick skin of the fruit covers a fairly thin layer of whitish, pulpy flesh surrounding a large, very hard central stone or 'pip'. The flesh is very juicy and has a bitter-sweet tang which becomes enjoyable when you get used to it, and a potent alcoholic beverage can be made by allowing extracted juice to ferment. A wide range of animals have a great liking for the dropped fruit, including baboons, monkeys and elephant. The fruit also makes a very tasty red jelly which can be served with meat or spread on bread. Many of the Park's staff bottle quantities of this preserve for use in those months when fruit is not available.

The bark is used by tribesmen to treat dysentery, diarrhoea and even malaria.

Mopane *(Colophospermum mopane)*. Rarely seen in the southern half of the Park, mopane suddenly abounds north of the Olifants river and – except in two relatively small areas north and east of Punda Maria – the entire area between here and the Limpopo is dominated by this tree. This dominance gives the northern half an atmosphere and appearance utterly different from that of the south. Vast areas can be

A massive marula tree *(Sclerocarya caffra)* spreads itself in Pretoriuskop camp. Right: Mopane tree *(Colophospermum mopane)*.

traversed where the mopane growth rolls in unceasing monotony broken only by an occasional herd of animals.

Yet this endless tract of vegetation generates its own beauty and fascination. The utter quietness so often experienced in mopane country provides moments of complete peace and solitude, a feeling of being a million miles from civilization. At other times, when thousands of cicadas unite in a high-pitched chorus on a cloudless summer's day and a herd of elephant stirs through the trees, kicking up clouds of dust, then you know you are truly in Africa's bush, that the scene could as easily have been enacted 200 or perhaps even a thousand years ago.

Over very large stretches north of the Letaba river, where they grow in shallow, poorly-drained soil, the mopane trees are stunted and only about two metres high. The best examples are found to the north, around Shingwedzi and Punda Maria. In the vicinity of Punda Maria dense forests of 15 metre-tall mopane can be seen from the road. The mopane's flowers are small, green and inconspicuous, and single seeds are borne in kidney-shaped, green pods about five centimetres long, which turn a biscuit-brown as they mature.

The leaves are very characteristic. Each is divided into triangular halves which together resemble a butterfly's extended wings. The upper surfaces have a bright glossy finish which enhances the attractive green.

Elephants are very fond of mopane vegetation and often can be seen lazily stripping trees of leaves or smallish branches. Being high in nutritional content, the mopane supplies most of the elephant's food requirements.

41

Top left: Sun-drenched Natal mahogany *(Trichilia emetica)*, and right: Nyala tree *(Xanthocercis zambeziaca)*. Cape date palms *(Phoenix reclinata)*, above left, fringe the Mphongolo river and, right, mlala palm *(Hyphaene natalensis)* in Letaba camp.

Natal Mahogany *(Trichilia emetica)*. This must be the most beautiful of all bushveld trees. Found along the banks of all the major streams and rivers, and about 20 metres high, it is one of the larger tree species, and is always well covered in dark green foliage. Because it provides abundant shade and has such a restful, pleasing appearance, this tree has been planted in most of the rest-camps.

The large leaves have a glossy, deep green upper surface and matt, pale green undersides. Clusters of green flowers generally appear in August or September. The round, hairy fruits, which to some extent resemble wild figs, ripen in January and February. Each green fruit has three compartments and splits open whilst still on the tree to reveal six very attractive red and black seeds.

The seeds are reputed to be poisonous, but are nevertheless avidly eaten by such birds as loeries and starlings, as well as by baboons and monkeys, none of which appear to suffer any side-effects.

42

Nyala Tree *(Xanthocercis zambesiaca)*. Common only in the Pafuri area, but occasionally found along the banks of most of the rivers and larger streams, the nyala tree is large and rather attractive. Specimens reaching 25 to 30 metres are not unusual, especially at Pafuri, and they are generally well clothed in a mass of fairly small leaflets.

Its clusters of small, creamy flowers attract large numbers of insects when it blooms in November and December. The tree drops a prodigious amount of green coffee bean-like fruits during autumn and winter. Inside the fruit is a hard, attractive, coal-black seed which people often collect to string as ornaments.

The fruits are eaten by a wide variety of birds and mammals. Despite each fruit having only a thin layer of edible matter surrounding the inner seed, monkeys, especially, are very fond of them. During March and April of some years, thousands of smallish green caterpillars virtually strip these trees of their leaves within a matter of weeks. When fully grown, the caterpillars descend to the ground on thin strands of silk secreted from glands in their heads. Once down, they seek out crevices in logs, bark or rocks to form pupae, eventually turning into attractive greyish moths. After such a mass descension of the caterpillars, a rather sorry-looking nyala tree appears to have giant sheets of silken webs draped from its uppermost branches.

The best examples of this tree can be seen along the road adjoining the Luvuvhu river at Pafuri.

Cape Date Palm *(Phoenix reclinata)*. Like the mlala palm, this species occurs throughout the Park, but is more abundant south of the Olifants river. Large stands are often found close to the water along streams, rivers and dams. In many of the smaller streams which only flow with heavy rains, the palms grow in the stream-bed, indicating that they are more water-loving than the larger mlala palm.

The Cape date palm tends to grow in clumps, though each tree has a single stem from which long, gently curving fronds radiate in all directions.

The fruits are shaped like coffee-beans and grow bunched along a series of ribs forming a fan. Baboons, monkeys and birds are very fond of these rather tasty dates.

The sap is used by local tribes to concoct an alcoholic beverage.

Mlala, or Fan Palm *(Hyphaene natalensis)*. Although not common in the south, mlala palms are fairly abundant north of the Olifants river up to the Limpopo. They grow in clumps, and several groups of these are usually found in a particular locality. Unlike the other species of palm found in the Park, mlala palms tend to be most abundant some distance away from rivers and streams.

Mainly as a result of veld fires, mlala palms are usually stunted or underdeveloped, standing about three metres high, though occasionally specimens 10 to 15 metres high may be found – especially in the far northern part.

The fruits are perhaps this tree's most obvious and interesting feature, dangling like oversized bunches of grapes from the upper stem. About the size of a child's fist, each young fruit is greyish-green but turns brown as it matures. Inside the husk is the grape-sized seed known as 'vegetable ivory'. Attractive but very hard, this is fashioned into ornaments by the local tribesmen.

Monkeys and baboons do chew at the husks of mature fruits, and elephants sometimes eat the young leaves and branches, but this palm is not a great favourite as a food source to animals. However, the sap is used to produce a potent intoxicating liquor. It is tapped from the stem and allowed to ferment for several days, or even weeks, before it is drunk.

Red Bush-willow *(Combretum apiculatum)*. Though not particularly striking or even attractive, this is a dominant species in many parts of its distribution range, being particularly common throughout the western half of the Park where it is probably second only to the mopane in numbers. Often multi-stemmed, it grows to about nine metres and seldom forms a well-rounded canopy. Instead, it sends out a number of fairly thin stems which in turn sprout a series of aimless branches.

Mature stems have a dark grey bark, cracked into a patchwork of elongate blocks. The leaves are tough and grey- to yellowy-green on the upper surface, paler on the underside. In spring, clusters of small yellowish flowers are borne on twiglets towards the end of small branches. The attractive fruits each have four thin 'keels' or 'wings', much like miniature Christmas decorations. They generally mature in autumn, when they become deep brown.

The extremely hard and heavy wood is excellent for making barbecue fires. In cross-section its grain is very beautiful, especially when polished.

A wide range of herbivores, including elephant, enjoy the leaves of this tree so it is an important food plant, particularly as it is so abundant.

Sausage Tree *(Kigelia africana)*. Like the baobab, the sausage tree is a great favourite of photographers. The large pendant fruits, borne so abundantly, give the tree so unusual an appearance that it seems like one of nature's experiments gone wrong. Though widespread, the tree has a preference for rivers and streams – as well as the high-rainfall area around Pretoriuskop, far away from the nearest permanent water. It is well shaped, with a spreading canopy of fairly large leaves, and can grow to about 20 metres.

The blotchy, light grey trunk, though usually fairly thick, does not reach much height before splitting to form the branches of the elegant and densely leafed crown. The large, oblong leaves, shiny green above but pale below, fall for a short period during autumn or winter, but at other times they provide fine shade. Flowers usually appear from July

Left: Scraggly red bush-willow *(Combretum apiculatum)*. Sausage tree *(Kigelia africana)*. (above right) and Sicklebush *(Dichrostachys cinerea)*.

to October as large, dark red, pipe-shaped structures which contrast splendidly with the surrounding leaves.

The pale grey-brown fruits probably need no introduction, and can grow to a length of 500 millimetres with a 100-millimetre diameter. With a little imagination, they resemble oversized sausages draped from the tree. The fibrous pulp of the fruit is tough and hard, which makes the 'sausages' rather heavy. Beware the animal below when these eventually drop! Baboons sometimes take a few hesitant bites, but soon discard the fruit, which is reputedly poisonous. Even the leaves appear to be shunned by herbivores. Tribesmen use the ground-up fruit to treat widely diverging ailments such as abscesses, rheumatism, and even venereal disease.

Sicklebush *(Dichrostachys cinerea)*. Closely resembling the acacias in general structure and appearance, this fairly small tree is also commonly distributed throughout the Park. It grows to a height of about five metres and consists of a bunch of fairly thin stems sprouting from below soil level. These stems subdivide some height above ground, and occasionally the trees become so abundant that they form dense thickets, impenetrable to man or other medium-sized mammals.

The seeds of the sicklebush are housed in pods which are long and twisted so that a group of them intertwine to form an unusual gnarled cluster.

Flowers, borne in mid-summer, are very attractive indeed. Brush-like, as in the acacias, they differ from the latter's flowers in that two distinct parts are visible – a beautifully pink basal part followed by a bright yellow section. This brush is, in fact, not one flower but a very large number of small flowers arranged around a central axis to form the inflorescence. The flowers making up the pinky-mauve basal part are sterile, whereas those in the yellow part are fertile.

Silver Terminalia *(Terminalia sericea)*. Visitors in the vicinity of Pretoriuskop cannot help but notice this rather nondescript tree which is not only the dominant species, but sometimes so abundant that it forms almost impenetrable thickets which exclude all other woody vegetation. The silver terminalia prefers well-drained soils and thrives in sandy areas such as those immediately north of Punda Maria, the Nyandu sandveld, and bordering the Lebombo mountains south of the Olifants river. Hardly any tourist roads traverse these areas so that Pretoriuskop is the only area where they can be seen in large numbers.

The tree may reach about 20 metres, although in most areas specimens vary between six and 12 metres. A single stem supports the rather well-rounded and densely leafed crown. The grey bark is fairly thick and cracked into a latticework of interconnected strips, much like those of the familiar acacia trees. Perhaps the most distinctive feature of this tree is the leaves. These are silvery- to grey-green on both surfaces and are long and narrow, tapering at each end. A fine layer of almost invisible hairs covers each leaf.

Flowers borne in October and November are each made up of many small florets arranged along a central axis in a creamy to yellow brush-like structure.

The central swollen section of the fruit is ringed with a wide, flattened 'wing' or 'keel' and encloses a single seed. As the fruit grows, it changes from green to an attractive red, finally turning brown before dropping to the ground.

The bark and leaves are used to treat stomach disorders, although some tribes believe them poisonous. Elephant and other herbivores such as kudu and giraffe eat the leaves and tender tips of twigs, but generally the tree does not appear to be a popular food source.

Tamboti *(Spirostachys africana)*. Plentiful throughout the Park, but particularly common around Skukuza, this fairly attractive tree generally grows about ten metres high. It is characterized by greyish-black bark, broken up into neat rectangular blocks arranged in rows along the stem to create a most pleasing effect. The wood itself, dark brown with pale blotches and streaks, can be used to make excellent and very beautiful furniture, though this is not a common practice – mainly because it is very hard, tends to be oily, and the sawdust is so toxic that it could lead to blindness if eyes are left untreated when touched by the dust.

The fairly small leaflets have a muted glossy-green upper surface with matt pale green below. Small, closely packed flowers form spike-like projections from the side of small branches and twigs, and are borne from September onwards. The seeds that follow have three compartments, which split into separate segments when they drop to the ground.

Tamboti seeds are heavily parasitized by small grey moths which lay their eggs in the still-developing fruit. As the seeds ripen, the moth larvae eat and grow so that by the time the seed drops to the ground they have hollowed it out entirely. Stimulated by the heat of the sun, these larvae flick their bodies, causing the entire seed to bounce into the air. On a warm day during seeding time, many of these 'jumping beans' can be seen bouncing about below tamboti trees.

Tribesmen sometimes use the bark as a purgative, but even with the very small quantities which they use for this purpose there have been several fatalities. Using the wood for fires is not recommended as the smoke causes headaches.

Thorn trees *(Acacia* spp.). The 25 species of *Acacia* in the Park form a very common and abundant group. All are well-armed with thorns which may be short and curved, or the formidable long, stout barbs which have caused many a puncture. The bark is generally thick, greyish and textured into a roughly broken patchwork of elongate blocks. There are exceptions, however, such as the striking fever tree *(A. xanthophloea)* which has a greenish-yellow bark peeling off in paper-thin strips.

The seeds, a great favourite as food for a wide variety of herbivorous mammals, are borne in long pods similar to those of the common garden pea, although flatter. Small beetles are very common in these pods as they eat their way through to the nutritious inner seeds.

Stand of silver terminalia *(Terminalia sericea),* left, and tamboti *(Spirostachys africana).*

The *Acacia* flowers are unexpectedly pretty. Many species have a small, rounded, delicately frail powderpuff-like inflorescence which may be bright yellow or creamy-white. Others have brush-like elongate flowers, again yellow or creamy. Flowers are abundant, so that the tree stands out brightly against a generally drab background.

Acacias are a very important component of the ecosystem as a large number of animals feed on them. Giraffe strip leaves from branches, totally ignoring the sharp thorns, which seem to have no effect on their tough tongues. Many insect species have found a home in acacias. As well as the small beetles which tunnel into and live inside the seed-pods, others burrow into the woody stems and gain nutrients by gnawing away at the very hard wood. Ants and solitary bees, too, have exploited these trees in a unique way. Having made a small hole in the large white thorns, they hollow out the insides as nests in which to lay their eggs and rear the young.

One of the most common species is the widely distributed knobthorn *(A. nigrescens)*. The tree may reach a height of 18 metres and very often has characteristic knobby protruberances on the stem. The pale white flowers of this species are elongate.

Transvaal Gardenia *(Gardenia spatulifolia)*. Few people notice this rather scraggly tree except during its flowering and fruiting. It is found in a very wide range of habitats, though never really abundantly, and grows to a height of about eight metres. The fairly dense rounded crown bristles with numerous spiky branchlets and twigs.

The rather short and squat stem is grooved and covered in a grey bark which flakes off in irregular-shaped blocks to reveal yellow underlying younger growth. Rumpled or undulating leaves are broad and round at the tip but taper sharply towards the axil. Fairly soft and pliable, they are shiny medium-green above, paler below.

Flowering may last from September to December and during this time the tree is a sight to behold. From near the ends of the twigs, long creamy-white tubes fan out into very attractive rounded flower-heads. Unfortunately, individual flowers are short-lived, lasting only a few days before turning brown and dropping.

Most conspicuous is the speckled-grey fruit, somewhere between a golf ball and a tennis ball in size. The ribbed covering gives it a segmented appearance, somewhat like a peeled orange.

The fruit is shunned by birds and mammals alike, and only a few herbivores have been seen plucking away at the leaves.

Tree Fuchsia *(Schotia brachypetala)*. This very attractive species, which tends to grow near rivers or streams, is found throughout the region, but more commonly south of the Sabie river. It is fairly large, often reaching a height of 12 metres or more. The deep green foliage which it retains for the greater part of the year, together with its large, rounded habit providing plenty of shade, makes the tree fuchsia one of the more noticeable and sought-after trees.

Top: Umbrella thorn *(Acacia tortilis* spp *heteracantha),* fever tree *(Acacia xanthophloea),* left, and Transvaal gardenia *(Gardenia spatulifolia).*

49

Tree fuchsia *(Schotia brachypetala)* (Photo: National Parks Board).

The rather small and leathery leaves are a shiny deep green above, but light green below. During August and September the entire tree bristles with a magnificent display of dark red flowers. These are borne in clustered florets and produce copious amounts of nectar which sometimes drip to the ground and attract a host of sunbirds.

The seeds are held in pods which resemble those of the acacias but are larger. In late summer the pods turn brown and burst open to release the seeds.

In his mammoth two-volume work on the trees of the Kruger Park, Van Wyk mentions that local tribesmen drink an extract of the bark to reduce alcoholic 'hangovers', while the roots can also be used for diarrhoea and 'heartache'.

The above are only a few of the trees to be seen. Because of the interest shown by so many visitors, Park officials have fixed numbers to a large variety of species. These numbers coincide with the National List of Trees, so that by checking against a list (which can be obtained in most of the camps) their names are easily determined.

The smaller flowering plants

I have always wondered why the smaller forms of wildlife are so constantly neglected or overlooked. Everyone knows what the elephant and the baobab are, and everyone wants to see them. But ask about the Buprestid beetle and the gloriosa lily; few will know of their exquisite beauty, yet they have a story to tell – of their lives and how they fit into the general scheme of things. Perhaps it is because we have an inherent concern for the power and size of living organisms, that the elephant and baobab top the list of viewing priorities for many visitors.

The Park nevertheless contains a multitude of highly attractive flowering herbs and shrubs, many openly exposed to view, others nestled in the concealing depths of shady forests, or snugly hidden between rocks or below overlying shrubby vegetation. They are there, abundantly so, we just have to look for them.

Strikingly beautiful when in full bloom during summer, the gloriosa or flame lily *(Gloriosa virescens)* is widely distributed in the northern regions. It often grows out in the open but seems to prefer slightly shaded environments. Using tree stems or shrubs as support, it clambers to just over a metre in height, clinging to its host with slender tendrils which curl out from the leaf tips. As a plant it is attractive, but when in flower this species stands out as royalty against its less-endowed herbaceous competitors. Each flower has six elongate

Impala lily *(Adenium obesum)*.

Barberton daisy *(Gerbera jamesonii),* left, and *Nymphaea* waterlily in bloom.

and well-separated petals which twist backwards and inwards, brilliantly exposing the rich colours, almost as flames leaping from a central core. The colour varies from plant to plant; in some it is orange, others yellow, yet others again, a combination of the two or a bright red fringed with yellow.

Scattered throughout the Park is the bulbous lily, generally known as the Sabie crinum *(Crinum macowanii).* As with many other lilies, a number of fairly long leaves sprout from the underground bulb and spread themselves open just after emerging from the soil. Like a periscope searching for signs of life there sprouts during spring, from the midst of these leaves, a stalk which erupts into a seductive spray of flowers in virginal shades of pink and white. Truly a beautiful sight, these flowers appear on flat patches of land generally after the first rains of spring.

The water-world also has its beauty to present, and here the multi-petalled *Nymphaea* species with their large and sedately floating leaves have no rivals. Flowering in summer, these very attractive waterlilies can be found in the quiet pools of many rivers and streams. The flowers vary from snow-white to pale blue, opening by day to play host to a number of insect visitors calling for a gift of nectar and pollen, then gently closing again for a night's rest.

Back on land, there are many other species to please a careful observer. More familiar to many people as a garden cultivar, the Barberton daisy *(Gerbera jamesonii)* grows wild on the banks of eroded dongas and ditches in the southern part of the Park. Here and there they may also be seen growing in shady places along the slopes of hills, especially in the Pretoriuskop area. Unlike their domesticated cousins which have been hybridised to flower in many different colours, these wild specimens bloom only in shades of red and yellow.

Sabie star *(Adenium swazicum),* left, and *Bauhinia galpinii.*

They have a long flowering period, generally from mid-spring to mid-summer.

Perhaps the most familiar plant to visitors because it has been so abundantly planted in many of the camps, and because it has such a typically 'bushveld' appearance, is the impala lily, *Adenium obesum* 'multiflorum'. These are normally seen as very thick-stemmed plants somewhat resembling a miniature baobab about a metre high, though occasionally they may reach three metres. From July to September large clusters of reddish-pink tubular flowers which end in a spray of white petals delicately bordered with brilliant red, embellish the stumpy branches. An exquisite bloom for a plant so essentially drab and which prefers to grow unadmired in the sun-drenched harshness of the bushveld world.

Of similar general appearance, but with a preference for the southern part, is the impala lily's sister species the Sabie star *(Adenium swazicum)*. It tends to be rarer than the former and flowers in summer, bearing delightful trumpet-like deep pink flowers grouped at the end of branches. These plants have also been planted in many of the rest-camps.

Among the larger or taller flowering shrubs, perhaps the most striking is *Bauhinia galpinii.* Many of these large shrubs with their mopane-like 'butterfly wings' can be seen growing in Pretoriuskop camp. The only area where *Bauhinia* appear fairly abundantly in wild conditions is around Punda Maria camp. Here, from February to April, large numbers may be seen, richly adorned with magnificent bunches of deep red flowers.

Visitors to the Pafuri area in September and October will be rewarded by the sight of masses of flowering *Combretum paniculatum,* otherwise known as the burning bush or flame creeper. Closely related to the robust leadwood tree, this creeping species drapes its snaking branches over low trees or shrubby riverine vegetation. Inconspicuous when not in flower, large numbers of these plants suddenly erupt in spring to create an almost festival atmosphere when their long rows of miniature crimson blooms cluster in elongate brushes along the sinewy branches.

Especially during spring and early summer, a myriad of smaller but highly attractive flowers is scattered throughout the Park. Most people overlook them as they gaze into the distance seeking lions and elephant. Their day would be so much more fulfilling and worthwhile if for once a conscious effort were made to notice the smaller things. From there the beauty will manifest itself and the interest grow.

ALOES

Many will have noticed or even photographed the aloes planted in most of the rest-camps. Letaba, in particular, has a large number adorning the entrance area to the restaurant complex.

Aloes are common, with several species spread throughout the Park, particularly noticeable on many of the hills and mountains. This genus of plants has adapted well to life under dry conditions. The leaves are thick and fleshy so that water taken up when the opportunity arises can be stored for long periods. A bitter-tasting component in the leaves discourages animals from feeding on the leaves, and as a further protective measure thorny spikes project from their surfaces. None of these discouraging adaptations protects the aloe from scale insects, however, and the often seen whitish or grey, powder-like layer covering part of the leaf is, in fact, many hundreds of scale insects clustered together. They live beneath a protective shield of wax which they secrete, and spend the major part of their lives in one position, sucking sap with their long mouthparts stuck deep into the leaf.

Despite their obvious adaptations to a dry climate, aloes have established themselves in a wide range of habitats. Some prefer rocky hills in dry areas, others open veld, some even prefer wet forest areas – they are found, in fact, in nearly all situations where plants exist. Among those found in the Park is *Aloe chabaudii,* a medium-sized species generally seen on the lower slopes of hills strewn with granite boulders, and which has greyish-green leaves. The lovely red flowers appear in winter.

A fairly large species which grows 2 to 3 metres high, *A. marlothii* occurs on hillsides as well as the open plains. The lower stem is covered with old, dried-out leaves which provide protection from herbivores. The deep golden flowers normally appear in early winter.

Aloe lutescens is medium-sized with light green leaves, edged with thorns and borne on a very short stem. It prefers to grow in open bushveld. The flowers, which appear in winter, are initially deep red, but become lighter and finally change to a pretty yellow when mature.

Aloe marlothii, left, and *Aloe chabaudii* (top right) are widespread, as are lichen-covered rocks (right).

LICHENS

Though few people realize it – walking or driving past without a second glance – lichens are one of the wonders of nature. Although it looks like a single structure, a lichen is, in fact, made up of two totally different life forms living in close association. Algal cells and fungal cells become inextricably linked in a symbiotic relationship, where the presence of each is beneficial and essential to the other. The fungus contains substances which dissolve nutrients out of the substrate it lives on, and contributes some of these to the algae in return for essential food. Together they make up the lichen.

Lichens usually grow on substrates where other plants cannot survive – on bare rocks, fallen logs or tree branches. Common throughout the Park, lichens take on many forms and colours and are often very beautiful indeed. Neglected by man, they nevertheless form part of the great web of life and contribute to its well-being.

55

Above: Flowering Natal red-top grass *(Rhynchelytrem repens)*.
Below: Bed of the Crocodile river choked with reeds *(Phragmites australis)*.

GRASSES

Grasses are a crucial component of any savannah ecosystem, for without them the whole system would collapse. It is not generally realized that in such an ecosystem grasses provide more edible material for herbivorous mammals than do trees, even where these are fairly dense. The major portion of grass is edible, whereas only the leaves, twigs, seeds, flowers and occasionally the bark of trees can be eaten. And because grasses grow closer together and cover large areas, they provide more food than the trees which appear to dominate them.

This is why so many grazing herbivores are found in the Kruger Park. All the large herds of buffalo, zebra and wildebeest depend exclusively on grass for food, while many of the mixed-feeders, such as impala, also consume considerable quantities. A simple calculation best illustrates how much food grasses do, in fact, provide. Taking only zebra and wildebeest into account and making a conservative estimate that each of these animals (about 21 500 zebra and about 8 500 wildebeest) only consumes grass equivalent to 2 per cent of its live mass on any particular day, one can calculate that approximately 191 300 kilograms of grass is being eaten by wildebeest and zebra *each day* in the Kruger Park.

Grasses are also faster-growing and replenish themselves more quickly than trees and shrubs, which makes it possible for them to support not only the herds of large herbivores, but also the possibly even larger demands from mice, other small mammals, birds, and especially insects. And, because of their very large numbers, insects consume tremendous quantities of vegetation, far more than is generally realized.

Veld-burning is one of the most important management practices and approximately 20 to 30 per cent of the Park is intentionally burnt every year. The most important reasons for this are to maintain the grasses in a luxuriant and highly palatable state for grazing animals, and to prevent the trees and shrubs from becoming too dense. But, like game-culling, this practice has sparked many a heated debate. Because grasses are so prolific and rapid-growing, so much dry material is produced at times that they snarl up an area, making new growth impossible and denying most other forms of vegetation, or even many animals, use of the ground.

Africa has always been a continent where fires, especially those started by lightning, are a regular feature. Over countless centuries, the African vegetation has had to adapt to these ravages to such an extent that periodic fire has become necessary to the existence of many vegetation forms. Rather than adopt the smothering attitudes of earlier conservation years, scientists now realize that fire is beneficial to the ecosystem as a whole. Periodic burning alleviates snarled-up areas and maintains the vegetation in a vigorous and stable state.

The obvious question to ask then is: Why not let Nature run its course and let lightning start the fires? The answer lies in Man's massive population explosion and his subsequent drastic modification of

Thatching grass *(Hyperthelia* spp and *Hyparrhenia* spp) crowd the open land between Sku-kuza and Pretoriuskop.

his environment. Only small patches of relatively undisturbed land remain on our earth, and the Kruger Park is but a minute fraction of an ecosystem which once embraced the whole of southern Africa. In times past it did not matter if an area the size of the Park burnt down completely in one fire, because the animals could move elsewhere for grazing, but this is not possible today – such a fire would be a catastrophe. Thus the whole Park is divided into blocks, some of which are burnt periodically, some of which are left undisturbed.

Grasses play a highly significant and crucial role in such other spheres as erosion control. Growing fairly close together, covering large areas, and having shallow radiating root systems, they hold the soil together and prevent its being washed away in the thunderstorm downpours which characterise the Kruger Park.

A very large number of grass species are found: some are tall, some short, some abundant and others very rare. One of the most striking species is tamboekie grass *(Hyperthelia dissoluta),* which is the dominant grass in the high-rainfall areas such as Pretoriuskop. Here it grows in large, dense stands producing robust vertical stalks up to two metres high. This species is often used for thatch, as is that actually known as 'thatching grass' *(Hyparrhenia filipendula).* Like tamboekie grass, it is a tall-growing species and common along the tarred road from Skukuza to Pretoriuskop. Although tough and often woody when mature, these two grasses provide good grazing for animals soon after a burn, when they are still young and succulent.

The well-known red-grass *(Themeda triandra)* is abundant on the open basalt flats or plains along the eastern region. Very palatable, it forms the staple diet of many of the larger herbivores. Vast stands of this grass – generally growing from half a metre to just under a metre high – cover the flat country adjoining the Lebombo mountains.

Natal red-top grass *(Rhynchelytrem repens)* is one of the more appealing grasses when seen in dense concentrations such as along the tarred road south of Tshokwane. It flowers virtually throughout the year, mature inflorescences forming a fluffy mass crowning the 300 millimetre-high stalk. When a patch of these flowering grasses is silhouetted against a reddening, late-afternoon sun it presents an unforgettable sight – bushveld at its best.

Growing exposed on the open plains, often on termite mounds, and very often in shaded areas below trees, is Guinea or buffalo grass *(Panicum maximum)*. Using tree stems for support, it sometimes grows more than two metres high. Being abundant and also highly palatable, it is often grazed by buffalo, zebra, and other herbivores with a preference for taller grasses.

All these grasses are found out in the open veld. However, the tallest species is found very abundantly next to water along the banks of all rivers and streams, often forming dense, impenetrable thickets. Scientifically it is known as *Phragmites australis,* more commonly just as 'reeds'. Despite its size – usually about three metres high – this is a genuine grass.

Buffalo and hippopotamus walking through the thickets of *P. australis* make characteristic tunnels and narrow pathways which are then used for considerable periods. Very few animals, except elephants, actually eat this robust grass, but birds such as weavers find it perfect as nesting sites. Hundreds of beautifully woven nests can sometimes be seen dangling from the upper parts of the reeds – often suspended above water and safely out of reach of the egg-scavengers.

Distribution and abundance of mammals

For an efficient management and conservation policy, accurate information must be available about the number of animals in the area to be managed or conserved. To this end the Nature Conservation staff at Skukuza annually survey the whole Kruger Park in a helicopter and light aircraft, taking counts of all the major game species and also observing the conditions of animals and vegetation in each area. In this way any sharp rises or decreases in population are soon noticed, and the cause or causes can be ascertained. Using the information gathered over a number of years, a pattern can also be established giving the general distribution and abundance of the various species.

In the following section, I have dealt with each mammal species separately for convenience and easy reference. However, it cannot be over-emphasized that no species exists independently of others in nature. Each animal, each species, forms part of a food-web where it eats other species of plants or animals, and, in turn, other animals feed on it. There is a constant dynamic interaction between the various animals. Any sudden fluctuation in the numbers of one species is likely to set up a ripple effect which will influence a large number of others in the food-web.

In describing the distribution of each animal species, I often refer to the south, central and northern areas of the Park. The southern section is the area between the Sabie and Crocodile rivers; the central area between the Sabie and Olifants rivers; whilst the northern area is that north of the Olifants river up to the Limpopo.

All the larger mammals and most of the smaller ones likely to be seen by visitors are discussed. The rats, bats, and some of the very rare mongoose species are not referred to, as they are unlikely to be spotted. For those who have a particular interest in these diminutive denizens of the veld – of which no less than 102 species have been recorded in the Park – an excellent guidebook by Pienaar, Rautenbach and De Graaff (1980), *The Small Mammals of the Kruger National Park,* is available in all the larger camps.

THE LARGER CARNIVORES

Lion *(Panthera leo)*. Lions remain, without doubt, the single species of animal which visitors most wish to see. All the hours and kilometres of driving under a hot sun are made worthwhile when confronted with the quiet dignity and raw power of these predators.

About 1 500 lions are scattered throughout the Park, but they are most abundant in the central district and around the Lower Sabie/Crocodile Bridge area. This coincides with the area most abounding in zebra and wildebeest which are their favoured prey.

This leopard patiently awaits the arrival of dusk.

A male lion in the mopane plains near Pafuri.

Although they occasionally make daylight kills, lions are mainly nocturnal hunters, preferring to laze under shady trees by day. Unlikely as it may seem, large animals such as buffalo and giraffe are frequently attacked and killed by these exceptionally powerful cats.

Research in Kruger Park has shown that lions are territorial animals, each pride having a fairly defined area in which it will hunt and live. They are normally found in prides two to six strong, although unusually large groups of 15 to 20 lions are seen occasionally.

When ready for mating, a male and female lion will withdraw from the remainder of the pride for several days, during which time they will couple repeatedly, neither hunting nor searching for food. The males especially become irritable and aggressive during this 'honeymoon' stage and need little provocation to attack any intruders.

The females give birth to between two and five cubs, but there is a high mortality rate amongst the young. An over-eager cub feeding at a kill among the adults may easily be clubbed aside by an irate male – often resulting in the ravenous youngster's death. In general, however, the cubs are well looked after. They may sometimes be seen playing affectionately with a resting mother, either snatching and pawing at her twitching tail, walking and rolling over her prostrate body, or quietly enjoying a maternal lick.

Leopard *(Panthera pardus)*. Leopards are nocturnal and only rarely active during daylight hours. They prefer riverine areas and craggy hills, although occasionally they may be seen out in open bush.

They tend to be solitary and spend their days resting on a comfortable branch of some tree or in a clump of thick bush. Despite their size, they are very good climbers and often drag their prey high into a tree, safely out of reach of hyenas and other scavengers. They do not appear to be very specific in their choice of prey, although impala are

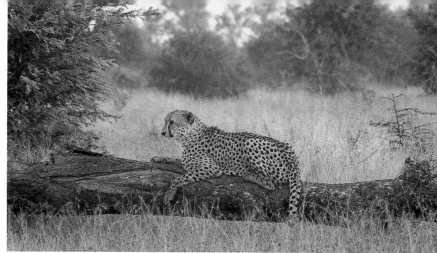
A cheetah warms itself in the gathering light of dawn.

frequent victims – probably because these antelope are so abundant and move to rivers in late afternoon when leopards become active.

Leopards are occasionally confused with cheetah, though they are more like domestic cats in build, with compact bodies, a relatively large head, and claws which are fully retractile. They do not have the black 'tear-marks' linking the eyes and sides of the mouth so characteristic of cheetah, and have 'rosettes' of circularly arranged spots along the side and back of the body.

More than 900 leopards occur in the Park, but are seldom seen because of their day-time resting and secretive habits.

Cheetah *(Acinonyx jubatus)*. Cheetah are plains-loving and shun densely wooded or mountainous regions. In open grassland with scattered patches of trees, they run their prey down in a short burst of very high speed. Cheetah have been known to reach speeds of 100 km/h in these generally short chases. To watch such a chase and witness the astonishing acceleration displayed by a cheetah intent on felling its prey, provides a scene few other larger predators can rival.

Generally encountered in groups of two or three, they roam over large areas and are found throughout the Park. Unlike leopards, they are more active by day, and also have solid black spots all over the body. Most characteristic is the black 'tear-mark' running from the inside of each eye down to the outside of the mouth. Lanky, streamlined animals, they are built for speed, having long thin legs, a relatively elongate thin chest and abdomen, and a head which is less bulky than that of a leopard. Not so obvious a difference is that cheetah cannot fully retract their claws.

Only 250 to 300 of these animals inhabit the Park, but despite their smaller numbers, they are often seen as a result of their diurnal activity and preference for open country.

63

Left: Social sniffing between a pair of wild-dogs. Top right: Disinterested, a hyena glances at a nearby impala, and (right) a black-backed jackal scavenges off a dead wildebeest.

Wild-dog *(Lycaon pictus)*. Reminiscent of cheetah in general build, the wild-dog also has long slender legs and a lean body – advantages to any predator which depends on its running ability to catch its prey. Sometimes called hunting-dogs, wild-dogs are found in packs of between five and twenty or more. Their large, rounded ears are very distinctive, as is their blotched or mottled body coloration, generally a mixture of black, orange-brown and white.

Nomadic for much of the year, wild-dogs will roam over very large areas, constantly searching for prey to satisfy their almost continuous hunger. Once the pack has chosen its next meal – usually an impala, zebra, kudu or other antelope – it hunts down the victim with dogged persistence and matchless stamina. From one point of view, wild-dogs may appear cruel, as they will rip and snap chunks of flesh from the fleeing animal as it gradually tires and slows. Once down, either from exhaustion or the extent of maiming, the animal's abdomen is ripped open by the assembled ravenous dogs. Death is very quick as they mill and throng to tear and rip chunks of flesh from any available part of the body. It is astounding how quickly – literally a matter of minutes – an animal can be reduced to a mass of skin and bones by such a pack.

When the pups are born the pack will cease its nomadic pattern and remain in the same general vicinity. The pups are left in burrows and adults return after a hunt to regurgitate meat for the youngsters to eat.

The 300 to 350 wild-dogs in the Park tend to favour flat country, but there is no particular area of abundance, except the broken country north-west of Malelane and the Malopene-Letaba river area.

Spotted Hyena *(Crocuta crocuta)*. Most people share mixed feelings of fascination and disdain for hyenas, whose appearance, with large rounded ears and a sloping back angling down from high shoulders to somewhat lower buttocks, is not particularly appealing. The thickset body is covered in a shaggy yellow-brown coat, blotched with black and dark brown spots.

Although hyenas live mostly by scavenging on the left-overs of animals killed by lions and other carnivores, they occasionally hunt and kill their own prey, and sickly animals or recently born infants are particularly susceptible.

Their large heads are so well supplied with thick muscles that it is easy to accept the commonly held belief that the hyena has the most powerful jaws of any animal of comparable size. With these jaws it can snap and crush bones with great ease; even tins, tyres and shoes inadvertently left outside camp are mangled almost beyond recognition.

Hyenas are fairly common throughout the Park, but are seldom seen as they spend their days resting in drain-pipes or tunnelled burrows. They tend to live in groups of up to ten, but are usually seen alone or as pairs. At night they emerge to look for food and water, often going hungry or having to cover great distances before finding something to eat.

Their melancholy and eerie nocturnal howls are commonly heard from most of the tourist-camps. Most familiar is the drawn-out 'Hooo-eeee-oooo' which may change over to frightful high-pitched cackles or screams. It is one of the most characteristic of African sounds.

Black-backed Jackal *(Canis mesomelas)*. This dog-like animal is easily identified by the black 'saddle' streaked with white, which contrasts strongly with the fawn-coloured coat covering most of the remaining parts of the body. Large triangular ears perch on top of a pointed face and the thick bushy tail is tipped with black.

Black-backed jackals are widespread throughout most areas, but are most common in the grassy plains south of the Olifants river. They are particularly active at night, scavenging the remains of dead animals or preying on newly born animals, mice, birds, eggs, and even insects. Usually solitary or found in pairs, these animals make their homes in burrows or protected rocky crevices.

At night their long drawn-out wails, interrupted by intermittent yelps, are often heard from most of the camps.

THE SMALLER CARNIVORES

Civet, Genet, Serval, Wild Cat and Caracal.

Several species of smaller cat- or dog-like carnivores are widespread and surprisingly abundant in the Park, but none of them is seen very often as they hunt and are active in the dark of night. Then they prowl singly, stealthily creeping up on any small creatures such as mice, rats, birds, lizards and insects. By day they hide in sheltered crevices, hollow logs, old burrows and tunnels, or in thick masses of shaded vegetation. A feature of many of these species is that, like leopard and cheetah, their shaggy coats are spotted and striped with bold camouflage patches and blobs of black and white.

The fairly large **Civet cat** *(Viverra civetta)* is common throughout much of the area, but has a preference for more open bushveld near rivers or dams. Civets are well-known for the strong smell of the secretions from their scent glands. Commonly known as musk, this se-

Large-spotted genet *(Genetta tigrina)*.

cretion is one of the important components of some perfumes.

The **Small-spotted Genet** *(Genetta genetta)* and the **Rusty** or **Large-spotted Genet** *(Genetta tigrina)* are also widely distributed, but are less common than the civet. Long-tailed and spotted in a way reminiscent of cheetah, these fairly small animals have a mass of about two kilograms and a shoulder height of about 150 millimetres.

Fairly large and with lean and athletic spotted bodies similar to cheetah, **Serval** *(Felis serval)* are very rare but nevertheless found throughout the Park. They prefer the more open grassland areas where they can see and catch their prey more easily.

Very similar to domestic cats in size and appearance, the **African Wild Cat** *(Felis lybica)* has a greyish body patterned with dark lines and streaks. They are fairly common and widely distributed throughout most of the vegetation zones, only avoiding the steep mountainous areas and densely overgrown forests.

Lithe and powerfully built, **Caracal** *(Felis caracal)* are rather large and have a shoulder height of about 450 millimetres. Characteristic long black tassles of hair curve outwards from the tips of the triangular ears, and the body is handsome in a fawn or red-brown coat, slightly lighter on the underside of the belly. Very effective predators, caracal will often chase and kill antelope larger than themselves, but more often prey on steenbok, duiker, rats and birds. They are widely distributed in most areas.

THE HERBIVORES AND OMNIVORES

Banded Mongoose *(Mungos mungo)*. This fairly small, hyperactive mongoose is easily recognized by the series of blackish-brown bands which run transversely across its back. As a whole, the rather long-haired coat is greyish and the grey tail tapers to a blackish point.

Active by day, banded mongooses are fairly common in most areas where there is a good cover of trees and grass, which protects them from the ever-searching eyes of eagles and other predatory birds silently gliding in the air above. They live in communal groups sometimes containing 50 or more members. The little animals scurry and scuttle around their chosen area, scratching and sniffing at a variety of objects which arouse their curiosity, to the accompaniment of a continuous mixture of subdued squeals and whimpers as the whole colony impatiently searches for food. They consume a wide range of edible items, catching insects, snails, scorpions, centipedes, millipedes and mice, and will happily chew away at fruit when the opportunity arises. If they find a nest filled with eggs, the front paws are used to fling each egg with surprising force between the hind legs against a solid object, so smashing the shell, and then lapping up its contents.

At night the entire colony holes up in a disused termite mound pitted with tunnels, in underground burrows, or occasionally in rocky crevices and jumbled heaps of boulders. If frightened during the day they streak for the protection of their concealing holes or crevices without hesitation.

Dwarf Mongoose *(Helogale parvula)*. As their name implies, dwarf mongooses are small, having a mass of less than one kilogram. Rather handsome with a uniform shiny reddish-brown coat, they live in communities whose numbers can vary from three to 20 or more.

Active by day, these elongate animals have much the same habits as banded mongooses. They are common in wooded areas, especially where termite mounds abound and fallen trees or rocky outcrops occur. In such areas they scratch for insects or a wide range of other small prey, running about with short rapid movements, interrupted by abrupt stops to peer inquisitively into the distance for signs of danger. They tend to make their permanent homes in termite mounds, while decaying logs or rocks are used as temporary hiding places.

African Elephant *(Loxodonta africana)*. Largest of today's terrestrial mammals, the African elephant has an adult mass of 6 000 to 7 000 kilograms. They are mainly grass, root, bark, and leaf feeders, each animal consuming vast quantities of this plant matter each year. To reach the succulent roots, elephants often push over fullgrown trees, causing devastation in areas where they are over-abundant. Because of their protected status, the elephant population increased to an extent where they posed a threat both to themselves and to other species. As a direct result of this, a culling programme has been introduced to decrease elephant numbers in areas where they are too abundant. This has stabilized the elephant population at about 7 500.

The average herd numbers about 14, although numerous solitary bulls are also found. Most elephant are concentrated in the mopane country north of the Olifants river.

Both males and females have tusks – although some have none – and those of the females tend to be thinner and smaller. The trunk, really an elongate nose, is an adaptation useful in many ways. Mostly it grasps vegetation when feeding, but water is also sucked into the trunk and then squirted either into the mouth for drinking, or over the body for cooling and cleaning. Unlike their hearing and sight, the elephant's sense of smell is very well developed, and they can sometimes be seen raising their trunks to sniff the air if danger or any other source of disturbance is suspected.

The African elephant's ears are larger than those of its Indian counterpart. They are rounded, flat and thin-skinned, with many blood vessels close to the surface, unlike the very thick skin which covers most of the body. By gently flapping their ears – something often seen – they set up a gentle breeze which allows heat exchange to take place through the surface blood vessels as excess body heat diffuses out through the thin skin.

Something of a legend has come to surround the massive old patriarch known as Mafunyane, 'the irritable one', who roams the far north of the Park in solitary existence. He has enormous symmetrical tusks, each more than three metres long, thrusting at a downward angle and

Top left: A banded mongoose scratches inquisitively to find a hidden morsel, and (right) a dwarf mongoose hesitates briefly before disappearing down a hole. Above: Near Shing-wedzi an elephant feeds contentedly on shrubbery.

forcing the huge animal to keep his head lifted high. Somewhere in Mafunyane's long history a poacher has tried unsuccessfully to kill this grand old man, the evidence plainly visible as a fist-sized bullet-hole in the top of his head. Park officials leave this elephant strictly alone, only checking at irregular intervals to see if he is alive and well, keeping his whereabouts a secret to prevent anyone molesting him. Mafunyane has only a few years of life left, but until he dies he will have privacy and remain king of his domain.

White Rhinoceros *(Ceratotherium simum)*. The terms 'white' and 'black' rhino are unfortunate and misleading, as there is no real colour difference between the two species. How the names were actually derived remains a puzzling question, though it has been suggested that the white rhino's name derives from the 'wide' – flattened or square – mouth, a good adaptation to its grazing way of life. It enables the animal to pluck and feed more effectively on the short grass which forms its main diet. By contrast, the black rhino is a browser, its pointed mouth adapted for feeding on leafy branchlets.

Although white rhino were once plentiful in the Transvaal Lowveld, they died out in this area late last century, as a result of excessive hunting and poaching. However, in 1961 biologists obtained a few of these animals from the Umfolozi Game Reserve in Natal, releasing them in a quarantine camp near Pretoriuskop. Since then many more have been re-introduced and released from the quarantine area. These translocated rhino established themselves so well and have bred so successfully that there are now more than 600. They are concentrated in the southern half, especially in the area between Pretoriuskop, Malelane and Skukuza.

Black Rhinoceros *(Diceros bicornis)*. As in the case of the white rhino, black rhino numbers were also dramatically reduced by excessive hunting in the last century. Tracks of the last living black rhinoceros in the eastern Transvaal were found in the southern part of the Park in 1936.

Again, as part of their policy to re-establish all the animal species which originally occurred in this area, the decision was made by the National Parks Board to re-introduce black rhino. In 1971, 20 of these lumbering beasts were obtained from the Natal Parks Board and released between Skukuza and Pretoriuskop. Since then many more have been re-introduced, so that today nearly 100 of them roam the southern and central areas.

Black rhino are somewhat smaller, with a mass of about 1 500 kilograms, and easily distinguished from white rhino by their pointed, elongate mouths. As browsers they prefer areas in which low, clumped acacia trees are found, providing both food and shelter.

Temperamentally rather unpredictable, black rhino are very easily provoked into charging. Thus it is advisable not to approach them too closely; they have been known to attack and bash vehicles.

Top: White rhino uses its flattened lips to graze. Above: Ill-tempered, a black rhino shows its somewhat pointed lips used for browsing.

Males and females of both species have 'horns', the foremost often much larger than the hind one, both being made up of normal hair that has fused. In the East, especially China, rhino 'horn' is highly prized as a powerful aphrodisiac. Rarity and demand as a result of this belief have led to extensive poaching of these animals.

This group of buffalo (top) appears docile, but can instantly change their behaviour. Young hippo (above) spar playfully in the Olifants river.

African Buffalo *(Syncerus caffer)*. Like oversized cattle blackened under the hot African sun, buffalo demand respect and are given a wide berth by most animals. Deceptively calm in outward appearance, aloof in attitude, there is always present a sense of latent strength.

About 25 000 buffalo are distributed throughout the Park where at least 90 herds each comprise more than 100 head and some exceptionally large herds number more than 600 buffalo. These very large herds are seen infrequently.

Numerous solitary males are found – generally wandering not too far from a river or waterhole – and it is among these that irate and vengeful buffalo occur. Especially if wounded in a mating fight, such injured single males readily charge any animal which disturbs them or rouses their suspicion.

Buffalo graze mainly on the coarser tufts of grass. Both males and females have horns, massive curved structures which serve as formidable weapons. Those of the males tend to be heavier and also wider.

Hippopotamus *(Hippopotamus amphibius)*. Largest of the freshwater mammals, the hippo reaches an adult mass of 2 000 to 3 000 kilograms and has a very thick hide and bulky, thickset body. A more ungainly animal than a hippo walking slowly on a river bank could hardly be imagined. Yet in water the hippopotamus is truly at home; its massive body supported to a large extent by the water, it moves gracefully through this environment and even swims when the need arises.

By day hippo are generally found in slow-moving, fairly deep parts of rivers, where they tend to congregate in groups of about five to ten, although as many as 70 or more may be found together. Males sometimes become very aggressive and domineering, resulting in vicious and lengthy fights, the loser of which is usually forced to leave the herd. Sharp canine and incisor teeth are situated at the front of the exceptionally large, wide mouth, and males can inflict severe wounds with these tusks. The pink-scarred skin of a beaten hippopotamus as it surfaces for air bears witness to the effectiveness of these weapons.

Hippo prefer to remain in or near water by day, and if suspicious or uncertain will submerge for several minutes, finally breaking the surface with a spray of water from each nostril. Often during the daytime wallows a male will bellow loudly, which may cause several other hippo to respond with similar deep-throated, staccato grunts.

At suitable sites hippo are frequently seen lying resting on a patch of clear sand adjoining the river. These well-rounded animals feed by night, leaving the water towards evening to forage on grass or small shrubs along the river banks, often covering considerable distances. Their dung is very easy to recognize, as they have the peculiar habit of 'spraying', or fanning, the dung against a shrub or tree.

Aerial surveys indicate that there are nearly 3 000 hippo in the various major rivers of the Park.

An adult impala ram chews contentedly on a mouthful of grass.

Impala *(Aepyceros melampus).* It is perhaps a pity that these animals are so abundant that their presence becomes monotonous and their grace and beauty tends to be ignored or taken for granted.

The most numerous of the medium- and large-sized mammals, with more than 150 000 impala occurring throughout the Park, they are particularly abundant in the central and southern parts. Commonly found in groups of about 10 to 30 head, there are nevertheless many herds which contain more than 100 of these agile antelope.

The herd structure varies according to the reproductive phase of the animals. The impala's mating season generally lasts from April to early June, and during these months bachelor herds will form. These are males incapable of securing their own small harem of females. During this mating season dominant aggressive males will fight fiercely with their horns, the two duelling opponents grimly facing each other with lowered heads, horns pointed forward. With sudden rushes they attempt to stab each other, but, almost invariably, the result is a loud clash of interlocking horns. Pushing and wrestling, they will attempt to unbalance each other. After a while they suddenly separate, their heaving chests fighting for air, acutely aware of each other and awaiting the next rush. Often, having done battle for a while, one of the males will sense that he is the weaker of the two and when an opportunity arises will turn and run. The victor will then gather a small herd of females with which he alone will have the right to mate.

After the mating season males become less aggressive towards each other, and the mating herds and bachelor herds break up to be replaced by mixed herds in which the two sexes intermingle peacefully.

In early November the first of the young impala are born, and lambing continues until about the end of December. Large numbers of these small but delightful impala can then be seen all over the Park.

Only the male impala have horns, and they also emit a loud, deep-throated raspy sound which serves to alert the herd. Readied by this warning, the animals will scatter at the least further sign of danger, leaping over shrubs or other obstructions. Occasionally when startled they may run across roads and give displays of very high and graceful bounds, often without any obstruction or other obvious reason to do so.

Steenbok *(Raphicerus campestris).* Shy and retiring of habit, these diminutive fawn-coloured animals must surely be the most graceful and dainty of all antelope. Slender-legged and with sharp-featured faces, steenbok are generally found in pairs scattered throughout the open bushveld, especially where the grass cover is fairly short. Here they will scratch around and nibble tasty bits of vegetation close to the ground. They are territorial animals and restrict their movements to an area they have marked with a secretion from a scent gland below each eye.

Because they are small and their body colour blends so well with their grassy habitat, steenbok are normally seen only when they stand fairly close to the road. Quietly feeding with slow deliberate movements, occasionally walking a short distance with delicate and elegant ease to a fresh patch of vegetation, they never fail to evoke a sense of innocence and well-groomed beauty. Only the males have horns, short straight projections directed slightly backwards.

Distributed throughout most of the area, steenbok are the most common of the smaller antelope, and are best seen from roads winding through the open bushveld between the Sabie and Olifants rivers.

Common, or **Grey Duiker** *(Sylvicapra grimmia).* These apprehensive little antelope are widespread throughout most areas, but are not often seen. At the first hint of danger they streak away with a characteristic erratic run punctuated by short bouncy leaps.

In size and shape duikers are very similar to steenbok, but can be recognized by their more greyish-brown hide and the short black crest of hairs between the short horns which project straight up from the top of the male's head.

Duiker prefer more thickly wooded country such as that offered by the riverine forests, and acacia/bush-willow/marula-covered areas in the south, where they are more common than in the mopane-dominated open plains. In their chosen habitats they browse contentedly on leaves during early mornings and late afternoons, lying up in shaded clumps of vegetation during the midday heat. They are normally seen singly, very rarely as a pair. Only the males have horns.

Sharpe's Grysbok *(Raphicerus sharpei).* Very shy and rare, these solitary little antelope are roughly the size of steenbok or grey duiker, though they are more squat or stocky and have a reddish-brown coat streaked with narrow splotches of white. The back has a characteristic hunched appearance and males have short stubby horns.

Sharpe's grysbok occur in many places north of the Sabie river, but are more common in the taller mopane woodlands north of the Olifants river. As they feed mainly at night, browsing or grazing as the opportunity arises, they are seen only infrequently. By day they rest in the protective cover of tall grass or beneath the shady canopy of shrubs. Like grey duiker, these attractive antelope are very timid and dart off into the concealing depths of the bush at the first sign of anything unusual.

Klipspringer *(Oreotragus oreotragus).* Poised like statues frozen atop the rocks and boulders which litter many of the granite hills dotting the otherwise endless plains, these extraordinarily dainty and handsome animals never fail to evoke an exclamation of surprise and admiration from visitors confronted with the sight. Klipspringers are one of nature's oddities, for they prefer to live in the desolate hills away from the conglomeration of other antelope species which compete for food on the open plains. Here amidst and on the rocks, they browse on the shrubs and trees which share their rugged home.

Translated from Afrikaans, the name means 'rock-jumper', a per-

Steenbok, top left, and klipspringer. Above: Sharpe's grysbok and (right) grey duiker
(Photo: National Parks Board)

fect description of this graceful antelope which leaps fearlessly from boulder to boulder with nimble ease. Fairly small animals with a yellowish-grey coat, only the males have short, straight, upward-pointing horns. Klipspringer are usually found singly or in pairs. They are distributed widely, but are relatively uncommon and not often seen.

Bushbuck *(Tragelaphus scriptus)*. These attractive, medium-sized antelope inhabit the lush riverine forests which adjoin most of the more permanent rivers. Shy and secretive, they rarely spend more than a few seconds in full view before disappearing with quiet stealth into the undergrowth which conceals them from admiring eyes.

77

Juvenile male bushbuck (left) and female nyala.

Poised motionless in the shaded vegetation below tall riverine trees, bushbuck are often difficult to see because of their coloration which melts into the shade, and the stripes and spots which break the body outline. Although individual markings vary, males tend to have white marks on the neck, legs and flanks, overlaid on a dark brown background colour. Females have similar markings, but their coats are usually not as dark as those of the males, and vary from fawn to a rich red-brown. Males have short pointed horns, usually less than 300 millimetres long, twisted in a light spiral.

Bushbuck are widespread, living individually or in groups of two or three, browsing on the plentiful vegetation of their habitat. While it is difficult to form a reliable estimate of their numbers, they are frequently seen and are especially common along the roads which wind along the Luvuvhu river in the Pafuri area.

Nyala *(Tragelaphus angasi)*. Although often confused with kudu, which they vaguely resemble, there are obvious differences which allow easy recognition of the two species. Nyala are somewhat smaller and more gaunt or thin, while the coats of the females are basically a rich red-brown and those of the males dark brown, compared to the washed-out grey-brown of kudu. Females and younger males have a series of up to eight lighter vertical stripes along the side of the body. Male nyala have a characteristic yellowy-orange on the lower parts of the legs, much as though wearing bright, knee-length socks. When the males are full-grown their lyre-shaped horns, which are white-tipped, reach only about half the length of those of kudu. Females of both species lack horns.

Nyala are rare and seen only at a few select locations. A small population of 30 to 40 is scattered along the banks of the Sabie river. Other small, isolated herds live along the eastern half of the Olifants, the Letaba, the Shingwedzi and the Mphongolo rivers and in the tall mopane woodland around Punda Maria. Only in the luxuriant riverine forest adjoining the Luvuvhu and Limpopo do nyala become abundant. Here visitors are certain to see these magnificent animals.

Male waterbuck (left) and roan antelope.

Waterbuck *(Kobus ellipsiprymnus).* As their name suggests, waterbuck are usually found close to permanent sources of water such as rivers or large dams, where they seem partial to broken country. These big antelope have shaggy grey coats, but their most distinctive feature is the large white circle which runs around their rumps.

Males have long rippled horns sweeping gently upwards and forwards in a shallow arc. Posed against a river background, such full-grown bulls form a magnificent picture of self-assured strength and dignified grace. Waterbuck are mainly grazers although they will often feed on leafy bits of vegetation as well.

Aerial census results show that more than 4 000 of this species are distributed throughout the Park. Herds – usually one or two males with several females – are consistently seen at the Shiloweni and Orpen dams near Tshokwane, and the Shawu and Kanniedood dams on the way to Shingwedzi. The banks of the Letaba and Olifants rivers are also very good areas for sighting waterbuck.

Roan Antelope *(Hippotragus equinus).* Fairly large, with a greyish or reddish-brown body and characteristic white and black markings on the face, roan antelope are one of the rarest animal species in the Park. Their long, pointed ears can be swivelled in almost any direction to locate the faintest of sounds which may mean danger. Both males and females have fairly long horns which curve gently backwards and are rippled or ringed for most of their length.

There are about 380 of these animals, generally living in herds of three to ten, although herds of 20 or more are occasionally seen. Most roan antelope are found north of the Olifants river up to the Luvuvhu, grazing in the open mopane plains. They dislike dense woods.

Roan are particularly susceptible to the bacterial disease anthrax. Sporadic outbreaks, which occur in especially dry years, pose a serious threat to the small roan population. To protect them, each year the research and management staff immunize a large proportion of roan. After a helicopter has found the various herds, a specially adapted rifle is used to dart the animals from the air with the vaccine.

Sable Antelope *(Hippotragus niger)*. Poised with majestic bearing and attired in a formal coat of resplendent black and white, the sable antelope is unmatched by any other animal for sheer grandeur and magnificence. A large, truly noble antelope, it is somewhat higher at the shoulders than at the rump and its strong neck proudly supports the great sweeping horns. These thick and formidable weapons are curved back over the body in an imposing arc, rippled by indented rings for the greater part of their length. Females have shorter horns, not as strongly curved as those of the male.

Full-grown males have a shining black coat with strongly contrasting pure white areas on the belly, rump and face. Females are more variable, but a glossy chestnut-brown tends to dominate in their coats. Immature animals are generally light brown.

About 1 900 sable are distributed throughout the length of the area, in open bushveld away from the dense forests or sparsely covered plains. They feed on both leaves and grass and are usually found in herds of up to 30.

The gravel road which travels past the Hlangulene and Mzanzene picnic-sites, the circular drives around Pretoriuskop and the road between Phalaborwa and Letaba are ideal for sighting herds of sable.

Tsessebe *(Damaliscus lunatus)*. With long legs and a jaunty appearance, tsessebe are reputed to be the swiftest of the African antelope. A lean athletic body slopes from the high shoulders to the somewhat lower buttocks. The body is a rich plum-brown but there are blackish-brown patches on the face, shoulders and lower rump. Short rippled horns which curve outwards from the head are a feature of both sexes.

Tsessebe prefer the grassy plains and open mopane-scrub country to the north of the Letaba river. The bulk of the roughly 900 population can be found in this area, although scattered herds roam as far south as Pretoriuskop. They are grazers, generally found in herds between two and 20 strong, and often mix with groups of zebra and wildebeest.

The gravel road between Letaba and Shingwedzi, which passes the Shawu and Hlamfu dams, is very good for seeing tsessebe.

Eland *(Taurotragus oryx)*. With a mass of about 650 kilograms – double that of kudu – these are by far the largest of the Park's antelope. Thickset to a point of appearing overweight, they have a characteristic hump at the shoulder and a broad fold of skin dangling loosely below the neck. The body is covered with a short-haired yellowy-brown or fawn coat, often with faint white vertical lines down the sides of the abdomen. Both sexes have moderate-sized horns, twisted into a spiral near the junction with the head. Females tend to have thinner and sometimes longer horns than males.

Of the roughly 600 of these animals, the great majority are found north of the Letaba river up to the Limpopo. A few scattered eland are known to live in the southern part, even as far south as Pretoriuskop, but are very rarely seen.

Top left: Sable antelope (Photo: Ian Espie) and (right) tsessebe. Above: Eland (Photo: National Parks Board).

Eland, which roam over very wide areas, prefer the open mopane plains or sandy woodlands, generally being found in groups of four or five, but occasionally merging to form large herds of more than 100. They are browsers and grazers, feeding on both leaves and grasses as the opportunity, or whim, arises.

The eland in the Park take flight at the first sight of cars, and their reluctance to remain near the tourist roads, combined with relatively low numbers, make them very difficult to see. The road from Shingwedzi to Pafuri, passing the Elandskuil and Mandadzidzi windmills offers the best chance to see these antelope.

Top left: Burchell's zebra, and (right) giraffe. Above left: Blue wildebeest and (right) kudu bull.

Burchell's Zebra *(Equus burchelli)*. This is the only species of zebra to be found in the Park. Black stripes completely circumvent the body, and definite light brown 'shadow-stripes' occur between the more bold black bands. These body markings are not in a set, invariable pattern. Each zebra's marking varies to a lesser or greater degree from the next and sometimes these pattern differences are quite striking.

Zebra have no horns. They are gregarious animals generally seen in groups of five to 30, grazing in association with wildebeest, though larger herds are often found. Although distributed throughout the Park, zebra are most abundant on the eastern plains, south of the Letaba river. They prefer open, savannah-type plains and about 25 000 zebra have been counted – making them one of the more abundant of the larger mammal species. Lions prey on them heavily, recently born zebra foals being especially susceptible to attack.

Zebra occasionally give a very characteristic call which is rather unusual and totally different from the braying or neighing of the donkeys or horses these animals superficially resemble. The call is almost bird-like, a high-pitched "quank-quank" repeated several times.

Blue Wildebeest *(Connochaetes taurinus).* Wildebeest are gregarious, forming small herds each averaging four to eight animals, but often congregating in large herds of 100 and more. Both sexes have broad horns which project sideways and then curve upwards, rapidly tapering to a fairly sharp point. Lean, with long thin legs and broad necks, wildebeest are a uniform greyish-black, patterned with indistinct vertical stripes.

Like zebra, with which they are often found grazing, wildebeest prefer open plains not too densely covered with thorn trees and other vegetation. Such a habitat not only makes it easier for them to detect potential predators such as lion, but also enables them to run more effectively. Here they feed on short tufts of grass, avoiding the taller clumps.

They are most abundant on the eastern side south of the Letaba river. With zebra and waterbuck, they are the favourite prey of lion, and many are killed each year. More than 10 000 wildebeest are to be found in the Park.

Giraffe *(Giraffa camelopardalis).* In appearance giraffe are probably one of the most unusual of all Africa's mammals. Their excessively long legs and neck allow them to feed on leaves and seed-pods of trees at a level where they have no competitors amongst the other major herbivores.

Their patchwork body-patterns vary slightly though individual colour differences may sometimes be very obvious, some having unusually dark body patches whilst others are very light. The differences do not indicate different species, but merely represent the normal variation found in every animal species.

Giraffe are susceptible to attack by lion, and many are killed each year. The great cats jump onto the back of a fleeing giraffe, grab a firm hold and bite into the neck. These giants, however, are not an easy prey as a kick from a distraught giraffe can kill or severely injure any careless predator.

Nearly 5 000 giraffe are to be found in the area, generally in small groups of about five to ten. They are not common in the northern mopane section, but are frequently seen in the central and southern areas – particularly in the acacia savannahs.

Kudu *(Tragelaphus strepsiceros).* As browsers, kudu prefer areas quite heavily covered with low trees. They are found throughout the Park, generally in small herds comprising one or two adult males, two or three adult females, and one or more juveniles. Females have no horns, but adult males are easily recognized by their magnificent horns twisted into a characteristic spiral.

Large, rounded ears can be twisted in virtually any direction to locate sound. The white underside of a kudu tail, which is exposed when running, is claimed to enable members of the herd to see each other more clearly and so remain together when fleeing from a predator.

Males will fight for the privilege of mating and in a few instances dead kudu have been found with their horns inextricably intertwined, presumably having starved as a result of being unable to separate.

There are close on 11 000 kudu, most of them spread over the southern and central areas though they are also common in the far north.

Chacma Baboon *(Papio ursinus)*. A definite favourite with children, baboons – with their sometimes almost human behaviour and expressions – can provide endless entertainment, and the playful antics of young baboons can be particularly amusing.

Social animals, they are found in troops 10 to 30 strong, and a definite 'pecking order' determines the status of each member in the social hierarchy. Generally a dominant male, known as the alpha male, is the leader and has the best choice of females and food. Immediately below him follow a number of large aggressive males, who serve as the protectors of the troop. They will feed and roam on the outskirts of the community, always ready to warn or defend the others against danger. Lower down, in a more loosely arranged hierarchy, follow the younger males, females, and infants. Baboons higher up in the hierarchy, especially the older, surly males, generally will not tolerate any challenge to their authority or position by those of lower status. Exceptions are always found, however, and the infants can usually approach and play with the large males or any of the other members of the troop without fear of reprisal.

Highly intelligent animals, baboons have a very strong protective instinct towards their young. If an infant has been injured the members of the troop will rally around and carry it, never leaving it behind. When an infant is threatened or held by a predator, the large males will fearlessly charge and make desperate attempts to save it. The maternal bond particularly is very strong, and on several occasions mother baboons have been seen carrying babies which have been dead for several days – unwilling to accept the loss.

Males have a very loud, deep-chested 'whaa-hoo' bark, used either as a sign of assertiveness, to intimidate intruders, or as a warning of impending danger. On the other hand, young baboons have a high-pitched shriek with which they voice their fear when reprimanded or chased by another member of the troop.

Baboons are common and often found along the edges of the riverine forest adjoining the major rivers. Most of the daylight is spent looking for insects, berries, and other titbits on the ground. Occasionally they will climb a tree to forage for fruit, birds' eggs, or succulent twigs. Towards dusk they move closer to the river and spend the night resting on some comfortable branch high in a tree. Nocturnal disturbances are frequent, however, giving rise to a great but temporary hullabaloo.

Top: Chacma baboons busily grooming, and (above) mother and infant vervet monkey.

Vervet Monkey *(Cercopithecus aethiops)*. Like baboons, these monkeys are social animals and found in troops of 20 to 30. Much smaller than baboons, they have an ash-grey body and a black face.

They are particularly adept at climbing trees and jumping from branch to branch for, like other primates, their eyes are not situated on the side of the head, but have evolved to the front of the face, which allows accurate judgement of angles and distances. The vervet's long tail helps maintain its balance when performing such acrobatics.

Common throughout the Park, monkeys are most often found on the edges of riverine forests, and though they are more at home in trees, will often descend to play or search for food on the ground. Their diet is wide and includes insects, fruit, birds' eggs, berries and leafy shoots.

In a number of camps situated near rivers, monkeys have become very tame and will venture into camp to look for any left-over food from outdoor meals. Then good photographs are easy to take as the vervets are easy to approach.

Warthog *(Phacochoerus aethiopicus)*. Ridiculed and scorned by virtually everyone, warthogs are held in unenviably low esteem because of their somewhat repugnant appearance. With their massive knobbled heads in total disproportion to body size, they are undeniably unattractive but nevertheless well adapted to their particular way of life. Kneeling down, they use the toughened snout to scratch and dig for roots or to nibble at tufts of grass cropped close to the ground by the larger species of herbivore.

Warthogs have a sparsely haired greyish skin and peculiar fleshy lumps or 'warts' on the face. Both sexes have tusks which protrude from near the front of the head, those of the male being much larger than those of the female.

These pig-like animals, well-known for their strength and toughness, never hesitate to put up a fierce, relentless fight if cornered. Many dogs have lost their lives – and even leopards are known to have come off second-best – after being ripped open by the wicked tusks of the boars.

Warthogs are common in most areas and usually live in small family groups up to seven strong. At night they rest in the protective confines of tunnelled excavations, coming out by day to feed and drink. When threatened, they run for their burrows and enter rear-end first, tusks facing outwards to ward off any danger which may follow them.

The long, thin, tufted tails which are held stiffly upright when running are believed to serve as beacons so that the members of a group can see each other and remain close when running through fairly tall grass.

Warthog (left). The Luvuvhu river (right) with its lush forested edges forms the Park's most rewarding area for birdwatchers.

Bird-life in the Kruger Park

With its subtropical setting and wide range of vegetation types, a rich and diverse bird-life can be expected to occur in this area. And indeed it does – providing sanctuary to an unusually large number of bird species, many of which face extinction in other parts of southern Africa or have already been driven from their former breeding areas.

Like all animals, birds have adapted to particular environments, each species being able to live and reproduce optimally in the particular habitat to which it is best suited. Some live in hollow trees in open bushveld, others in elaborate nests delicately interwoven with reeds overhanging streams, whilst others again prefer the dense overgrown riverine forests. To each species his own food, nest and habits. The relatively few visitors interested in viewing birds, wherever they happen to be, will find a wide range of species.

Ostriches *(Struthio camelus)*. Weighing in at up to 150 kilograms, the OSTRICH is the largest of earth's surviving birds. To lift such an enormous body off the ground and keep it in flight would require an enormous expense of energy, so these birds have evolved a different strategy for survival. Their wings have become smaller – and are now essentially useless – whilst the legs have developed into powerful and muscular structures. In defence the strength of these legs becomes evident – the ostrich can run away from danger at speeds of more then 70 kilometres an hour, and, as a last resort, can deliver vicious, slashing kicks which will deter any potential predator.

Ostriches are not very common, but occur widely in the central and northern areas where they are occasionally seen in small groups of one or two males and a few females. The males have black plumage with contrasting white feathers ending off the wings, while the females are covered with unattractive, dirty-brown feathers. Ostriches avoid thick, densely wooded areas where it is not easy to see danger approaching and their running would be obstructed by bushes. On the open plains they scratch away and feed on plant material such as seeds, berries and succulent shrubs, now and then swallowing a pebble which helps crush unchewed vegetation in the stomach.

Females lay up to 20 eggs in a breeding season, depositing them in a simple hollow in the earth. Such a nest is a sight to behold, as each off-white rounded egg holds the equivalent content of 24 normal chicken eggs. Their shells are very tough and can support the weight of a full-grown man.

Males and females take turns in incubating the eggs, the black-feathered males sitting on the eggs at night, whilst the brown females, which blend very well with the soil and surrounding drab vegetation, keep the eggs warm and protected during the day.

Top left: Male and female ostrich (Photo: Ian Espie), and (right) darter. Above: Green-backed heron (left) and hamerkop (right).

DARTERS, HERONS AND HAMERKOP

Darters *(Anhinga melanogaster rufa)* must surely rank among the most elegant and graceful of birds. They are frequently seen poised silently atop some dead log or rock jutting from a large expanse of water, sitting quietly for hours on end. The long snake-like neck is held close to the body, occasionally craned when the bird is aroused by an unusual sound or spots a fish below. Although not very common, darters occur along all the major rivers and some of the larger dams or pans. They feed on fish and frogs, diving to catch their prey, sometimes swimming rapidly with only their heads protruding above the water.

Also found wading slowly and serenely in the shallower water of all the major rivers is the grey and brown **Goliath Heron** *(Ardea goliath),* largest of all the Park's heron species. It stands about 1,4 metres tall on long, spindly legs and has a long, gracefully curved neck. Very shy birds, they fly off when anyone attempts to approach them, so that binoculars are essential to get a close look at these handsome creatures. Their diet consists of fish.

Probably the most common of the herons is the small, but attractive **Green-backed Heron** *(Butorides striatus).* It is found along all the rivers and at many of the dams and pans, preferring to stalk the vegetation-covered edges for a wide range of food such as dragonflies, grasshoppers, butterflies, other insects, frogs, tadpoles, small crabs, spiders and fish. These herons walk with their long necks held tight against the body until a likely-looking prey is spotted. Slowly they creep up to the victim, then swiftly shoot out the long neck to grasp the morsel. Most green-backed herons are seen singly, although pairs are occasionally found hunting together in summer.

Cattle Herons or **Cattle Egrets** *(Bubulcus ibis)* are normally seen in groups of up to a dozen, and though not very common, they are found in open bush throughout the area. These dainty white birds with yellow bills often walk among herds of game, feeding on any insects showing themselves when disturbed by the hooves and movements of the animals. The egrets feed on a wide range of prey, which as well as insects may include lizards and young birds – or frogs, tadpoles, fish and crabs when they feed around pools or dams. In the evenings they fly to the top of dead trees or prominent vegetation to roost communally, providing a peacefully pleasing sight for visitors driving back to camp through the gathering dusk.

Of several other species of heron which are found in the area, perhaps the **Grey Heron** *(Ardea cinerea)* and the **Great White Heron** *(Egretta alba)* are most frequently seen. They are not common, but have been recorded at various localities throughout the Park. Both species are found near water, usually quiet pools in large river beds or at the edges of large dams where they stealthily hunt small water animals such as crabs, frogs, insects, fish, lizards and snakes.

One of the most common of the birds associated with rivers and dams in the Park is the **Hamerkop** *(Scopus umbretta).* In Afrikaans, the name means 'hammer-head', which, indeed, the head resembles. These fairly large, brown birds are frequently seen at many of the rivers and dams. They stroll through the shallows, sometimes pecking, sometimes tentatively kicking some underwater object, searching for frogs, fish, crabs, snails and insects on which to feed. They build huge nests in suitable trees close to the water, using sticks, reeds, branches and twigs to construct the dome-shaped structures with their entrances underneath. They may take six months to finish the work, but when completed few predators are able to enter or break the nest.

STORKS

Of all the larger birds found in the Park, the storks are a definite favourite of visitors. The largest, and perhaps the most strikingly beautiful, is the **Saddlebill** *(Ephippiorhynchus senegalensis)*. With its black and white body and red bill saddled with a band of black, it provides a display of regal splendour which draws admiration from those fortunate enough to chance upon this bird. Although fairly rare, saddlebills occur throughout the Park, along rivers and especially at pools of water in open veld. They are generally found singly or in groups of two or three, strutting around the shallows of pools, looking for any small creatures they can find to feed on. Females can be distinguished by their ring of yellow around each eye.

The **White Stork** *(Ciconia ciconia)* is common in summer and occurs in flocks throughout the area. Summer migrants, they return to Europe when the southern winter approaches. Large numbers are often seen walking slowly through open bush looking for food such as locusts and other insects.

Many other lesser-known and somewhat rarer storks are to be found, including the black stork, white-bellied stork, open-bill stork and woolly-necked stork.

An exception to the usual grace and beauty associated with these birds is the **Marabou Stork** *(Leptoptilos crumeniferus)*. Widespread and commonly found in flocks, these birds have an unusually repulsive appearance. The head and neck tends to be very sparsely feathered, which together with the sickly colour of the bill gives the impression of the bird being very dirty and distinctly unattractive. Marabou storks tend to be scavengers, feeding on decomposing offal and carcasses. They also often wade in shallow streams searching for frogs, crabs and fish, or stalk about on land hunting for insects and small animals.

HADEDAS

Hadeda Ibises *(Bostrychia hagedash)* are one of the better-known birds of the Park, being widespread and fairly common. Their loud, harsh 'Haaaa!' or 'Ha-ha-ha-ha-haa!' calls are heard frequently, when the birds are disturbed or when flying to their roosting sites in the evening. During the day they walk through the bush in groups up to 10 strong, hunting for small creatures such as insects, lizards and snails or even carrion and offal. They tend to remain in the general vicinity of water, but prefer not to feed on the very edges of rivers or dams. Their squat, elongate grey-brown bodies with shimmering purple-green on the wing-bases, and their long downward-curving beaks are familiar figures around many of the rest-camps. Three to four reddish-stained eggs are laid in a nest built as a platform of sticks in the branches of some tree not far from water. The male and female take turns in sitting on the eggs for just under a month, waiting patiently for their offspring to hatch.

Roosting marabou storks (left) and hadeda ibis.

DUCKS AND GEESE

Ducks and geese have the magical quality of lending an air of tranquillity to any pool of water they inhabit. Perhaps it results from the combination of attractive colours, their rounded, plump bodies, their habit of living in small family groups, and the quiet but boldly innocent manner in which they live and swim in the placid waters they have chosen.

The attractive multicoloured **Egyptian Geese** *(Alopochen aegyptiacus)* are the most abundant and widespread of these water-dwelling species and can be seen at any time of year in most of the rivers, dams and pools. Usually they are found in pairs, although occasionally large numbers may congregate in and around pools on the open veld. Walking slowly in the shallow water or along the bank, they search for soft and tasty bits of vegetation such as freshly sprouted grass, and algae. Egyptian geese seem to breed throughout the year, nesting in a variety of situations, often in thick vegetation near water or on the abandoned nest of a hamerkop. Fluffy chicks are frequently seen scurrying around the parents or slowly gliding on the water, always inviting another lingering look.

Largest of the water-fowl is the **Spur-winged Goose** *(Plectropterus gambensis)*. Summer migrants, individuals or flocks of more than 20 birds, colonize stretches of river or pans over the entire area from the Crocodile river up to the Limpopo. They prefer open expanses of water fringed with luxuriant grass or short vegetation where they can search for tasty shoots of plants, young grass and occasionally soft, fallen fruits. Except when breeding, they seldom remain long in one place, preferring to fly off seeking new pans, often stopping for a while at small, temporary pools formed by a shower of rain.

The **White-faced Whistling Duck** *(Dendrocygna viduata)*, named for the broad band of white running across the eyes and over the head, is one of the most handsome water-birds in the Park. Only present in summer, and rather rare, these birds are found in small flocks on many of the rivers and pans. They are most active at night, wading in the shallows in search of small water animals or seeking seeds along the banks. By day they either sleep or sit quietly atop some log or fallen tree, casting an occasional wary eye at some unfamiliar sound before settling peacefully again.

Knob-billed Ducks *(Sarkidiornis melanotos)* are among the most prominent avian summer visitors. The males, particularly, draw attention because of the large spoon-like outgrowth, which projects upright along the top of the bill, and their contrasting black and white body coloration. An omnivorous species, these ducks feed on insects and plant seeds on the edges of rivers or pans. During the rainy season they are fairly common in most areas, often being seen at pans or dams in the open veld.

About eight other species of ducks and geese spend part or all of their lives in the Park. Most only arrive in summer when rains have formed pools of water for them to inhabit; all are rare and not often seen. During the dry winter months these birds migrate further north into Africa in search of warmth, water and food.

Egyptian geese feeding in shallows of Luvuvhu river (left) and a pair of hooded vultures.

VULTURES

Vultures must occupy the most unenviable position in the animal kingdom. Loathed and despised by most people for their scavenging habits and dreary, dirty appearance, their ravenously greedy behaviour around a carcass unfortunately reinforces this opinion. Yet these birds perform one of the greatest services and are of enormous benefit to man – as sanitation agents vultures are undisputed masters of their art, effective beyond the ability of any other group of animals. By scavenging on dead animals they prevent a build-up of decomposing bodies littering the bush, decrease the possibility of outbreaks of disease, and assist breaking down and spreading the nutrients concentrated in a carcass.

Gliding high and with undeniable grace, they notice with uncanny rapidity any carcass; only those dead animals hidden in the riverine forests or covered with dense vegetation escape their extraordinary sight. Soon the first few drop from the sky to bounce closer to the bounty of meat. Other vultures notice their descent and converge on the scene, so that within a few hours more than a hundred vultures may be present at a single carcass.

Under normal circumstances a carcass results from any lion or other predator kill. In such cases the vultures will have to wait, impatiently, for the predators and any hyenas attracted by the commotion to finish their share before the birds can move in. When their turn comes, not much is left, so that much of a vulture's life is spent in a constant, hungry search for new carcasses. Their appetite is enormous, and with so much competition from other vultures, it is not surprising that any carcass lying in open veld is very soon stripped of any available flesh. Animals such as impala or kudu dying from disease are very soon discovered by vultures, and by their effort alone, without the help of hyenas or jackals, the vultures will rip and tear the carcass apart until, within a matter of hours, all that remains is a bare skeleton with perhaps a few strands of skin dangling from the bones.

Watching a group of vultures around a carcass is fascinating and sometimes entrancing. The number of vultures which can fit on and around any body is limited, so that there is a continuous jostling for position – some crawling right into the hollowed-out abdominal cavity, others threatening and fighting each other to get at the meat, and most engaged in a frenzied rush, with razor-sharp beaks pulling and tugging at the remains before they are chased away by new arrivals. Standing around are the earlier arrivals, so heavily gorged that they have difficulty trying to fly. All the while there is the sound of flapping wings – of vultures flying in or leaving, or simply flapping to vent frustration and anger – and the sound of raw flesh being ripped and torn to satisfy an impossible collective hunger.

Most vultures fly enormous distances during their search for food. Many hundreds of kilometres are covered in this way each week, so that a lack of nests in a particular area does not mean vultures do not

A magnificent fish eagle displays the vivid plumage which makes it one of the most striking of African raptors.

use that area. The nest serves as a rearing place for the young, but food is rarely available nearby. The adults will return to the nest and regurgitate some of the food they have eaten, occasionally including a few bits of bone which supplement the intake of calcium by the chicks, a prime requirement for their own bone-growth.

By far the most abundant of the six species occurring in the Park is the **White-backed Vulture** *(Gyps africanus)*. They are brown in overall plumage with pale undersides, and the adults have a characteristic pale off-white patch on the back which is only visible when the wings are spread. They are often confused with Cape vultures but lack the yellow eyes of the latter species. White-backed vultures usually form the bulk of the scavenging birds around any carcass. Several have been found nesting in the Park, making their untidy nests in the topmost branches of acacia trees near rivers.

Largest is the **Lappet-faced Vulture** *(Torgos tracheliotus)* and, as befits its stature, it has the garb and dignified behaviour of a monarch. Covered with dark brown feathers which contrast well with the bare, bright red skin of the proud neck and head, this bird, sometimes referred to as the 'King Vulture', has a wing span of more than 2,7 metres. Lappet-faced vultures are common but never abundant, generally being seen in twos or threes at a carcass. When they arrive the other vultures scatter in deference to the size and strength of this bird. Slowly they will approach the carcass and calmly feed until satisfied; only then will the other vultures return to resume their mad attack on the decomposing flesh. Lappet-faced vultures also breed in the area, making their large flat nests in the tops of trees and laying a single egg per breeding season.

Other vultures which occur in the Park are the **Cape Vulture** *(Gyps coprotheres)*, **White-headed Vulture** *(Trigonoceps occipitalis)*, **Egyptian Vulture** *(Neophron percnopterus)* and the **Hooded Vulture** *(Necrosyrtes monachus)*.

HAWKS AND EAGLES

A wide array of raptors is found throughout the Park and causes visitors considerable confusion and frustration, for many of these birds appear very similar to all but an experienced birdwatcher. Hawks and eagles form the bulk of all the large birds of prey which feed on animals such as frogs, lizards, snakes, other birds, small mammals and even fish.

The **Fish Eagle** *(Haliaeetus vocifer)* with its melancholy call is widely regarded as representing the spirit of Africa. Certainly this handsome bird, with its graceful flight and drawn-out lonesome call, evokes a feeling of admiration in all who see it. Fish eagles are fairly common along all the major rivers and are generally seen in pairs or singly, either perched in a tree near a river or soaring in search of prey. As well as fish, which they catch by scooping them from the water, they prey on small creatures such as mice or birds.

Rivalling the fish eagle in beauty and grace is the majestic **Bateleur** *(Terathopius ecaudatus)*, king of the open bushveld. The bateleur is common and spends much of its time gliding in search of prey. Any small creature, including snakes, birds and animals killed on the road by fast-travelling vehicles, is also a welcome meal.

Yet another widespread and fairly common large bird of prey is the **Martial Eagle** *(Polemaetus bellicosus)*. The characteristic white front spotted with brown makes this species easy to identify. These eagles prefer open bushveld, and hunt animals such as rabbits, squirrels, monkeys and birds. Martial eagles are often seen perched at the very tops of high trees. Like most other hawks and eagles, they tend to be solitary.

Other common birds of prey which occur in the Kruger Park are the tawny eagle, Wahlberg's eagle, the brown snake-eagle, and the little banded goshawk.

FRANCOLINS

The five species of FRANCOLIN living in the Park are very similar in habits and appearance. All are a soil-coloured overall brown, streaked and blotched with light and dark shading which provides ideal camouflage in their preferred grass-covered open bushveld environment. Here they are found in pairs or small groups, searching for plant seeds, bulbs or insects and other small creatures. They are very much ground-loving birds, running rapidly through the grass when alarmed, rather than flying. Often when sensing oncoming footsteps, they will remain frozen, depending on their camouflage to fool the intruder. Sometimes they fly up with angry, raucous calls just before being stepped on. They nest in shallow depressions under a bush or obscured among a clump of grasses, and four to nine pale, often speckled, eggs are laid. The fluffy little chicks have such good camouflage colours that when they lie quietly, as they do when danger is suspected, it is very difficult to see them.

Swainson's francolin (left) and crowned guinea-fowl.

Swainson's Francolin *(Francolinus swainsonii)* and the **Natal Francolin** *(Francolinus natalensis)* are the most abundant and widespread of the species. They are often seen at the roadside, calmly pecking away at old elephant dung in search of insects, and regularly casting a wary eye at the visitor until they scuttle into the undergrowth if they feel threatened. **Coqui Francolin** *(F. coqui coqui),* **Crested Francolin** *(F. sephaena),* and **Shelley's Francolin** *(F. shelleyi)* are all rarer and localized in their distribution, but are often seen by visitors driving through their chosen habitats.

GUINEA-FOWL

Two species of guinea-fowl are found: **Crowned** *(Numida meleagris)* and **Crested** *(Guttera pucherani).* Crested guinea-fowl are very rare and the only area where they are likely to be seen is at Pafuri along the road winding parallel to the Luvuvhu river. They are communal birds, preferring overgrown bush adjoining rivers, and feed on fruit, seeds and insects. They are easily recognized by the characteristic tuft of irregularly directed black feathers on top of the head.

Crowned guinea-fowl are common and widely distributed, especially in the vicinity of rivers or other sources of permanent water. Like crested guinea-fowl, they are gregarious and live in communities. Although they fly well and for considerable distances, they prefer running from danger.

JACANAS AND BLACK CRAKES

These fairly small, highly attractive birds are found along most of the rivers, quietly strutting about the shallows with long jerky strides. Where floating vegetation occurs, they confidently bounce around on the lily-pads or knotted masses of reeds, using their extraordinarily long toes as a wide platform for support. Most of their time is spent in a continuous search for insects, snails, tadpoles, and such tasty bits of vegetation as seeds. Occasionally they will suddenly take to the air and with rapid wing-beats and a final graceful glide skim low over the water to feed at another site.

The **African Jacana** *(Actophilornis africanus)* is one of the most beautiful of our birds associated with water. The greater part of the body is covered with reddish-brown feathers while the under-surface of the neck has a very appealing yellowy-orange patch. Long, stilt-like legs with elongate toes raise the body well above the surface of the water so that the bird can see better and move more easily.

The **Black Crake** *(Amaurornis flavirostris)* is even more striking in its strongly contrasting colours. With a pitch-black body, the bright yellow beak and crimson legs are admirably distinctive. They are more shy than jacanas and usually remain close to the reed-fringed edges of the river, where they will quickly disappear into the shadows when frightened.

Black crake (left) and blacksmith plovers.

PLOVERS AND WADERS

A fairly large group of birds and often difficult to identify, they are mostly plumaged in drab patterns of white, brown and black, though a few are very attractive with bold, eye-catching markings. Most of the species are associated with water, generally strolling around the shallow parts or on the banks adjacent to marshes, dams or rivers. They have rather long legs and the plovers generally move with conspicuous short, jerky runs. Their diet consists of insects, worms, tadpoles and other small animals. Many of the plovers commonly breed in shallow depressions ringed with sticks and stones, but virtually all the waders breed in the northern hemisphere during our winter. With spring many thousands of these birds return to enjoy the abundant food and water.

Blacksmith Plovers *(Vanellus armatus)* are the most handsome of the various species. Strikingly patterned with patches of white, black and grey, these birds are widespread and fairly common around permanent sources of water. They are usually seen in pairs or small groups, restlessly moving through open grassy areas especially around dams or pans.

Crowned Plovers *(V. coronatus)* are also fairly common and widespread, but prefer dry overgrazed bushveld areas, often far from water. The top of the head is black with a prominent white ring while the chest and back are a uniform sandy-brown. Red legs also characterize this species. Usually seen in pairs or small groups, they run around the veld with heads depressed and bodies held low to the ground, suddenly stopping and stretching up to peer intently at their surroundings. The bulk of their diet consists of insects.

Several other species of plover are found in the Park, but they tend to be rare and limited in their distribution.

Of the various species of wader only three are widespread and fairly common, except during winter when they migrate elsewhere in Africa and to Europe. The so-called **Ruff** is the male of *Philomachus pugnax,* the female being known as a reeve. The species is known collectively as ruff, and flocks are usually seen near dams and pans. Ruffs have white undersides with boldly mottled, brownish backs.

The **Common Sandpiper** *(Tringa hypoleucos)* is usually found singly or in pairs near rivers, streams or dams. White below but dark brown above, they have a definite patch of white which extends up each shoulder as irregular epaulettes. The under-surface of the neck is light brown, streaked with darker lines. They have a delightful habit of bobbing the rear of their bodies up and down while ambling through shallow water in search of small animals.

Wood Sandpipers *(T. glareola)* are usually seen singly, feeding at the edges of streams, dams and temporary grass-filled pools. A brown back is conspicuously speckled with white, and a band of white runs from the bill over the eyes.

DIKKOPS, KORHAANS AND KORI BUSTARDS

Although fairly common, the two species of dikkop are not frequently seen. Their predominantly brown bodies are marked with dark speckles and stripes, an inconspicuous coloration which, with their habit of resting under bushes or in clumps of grass by day and becoming active only at dusk when their search for insects and other small creatures begins, contributes to their invisibility. The **Water Dikkop** *(Burhinus vermiculatus)* prefers the bush-covered areas around permanent sources of water such as rivers and large pools, and is easily distinguished from the dry plains-loving **Spotted Dikkop** *(B. capensis)* by a pale band, bordered above with black, which runs horizontally across the body when the wings are folded. Other than their preference for different habitats, the two species are of similar behaviour – resting by day, preferring to run snake-like through the undergrowth when disturbed rather than fly, and feeding during twilight or at night. Both species usually lay two pale eggs, blotched with brown, in shallow depressions in open veld or under shrubs and bushes.

Similar in general body colour, size and shape to the dikkops, the two species of korhaan found in the Park can be distinguished by their smaller heads and longer necks. The **Red-crested Korhaan** *(Eupodotis ruficrista)* prefers fairly dense bushveld areas, while the **Black-bellied Korhaan** *(E. melanogaster)* is normally found in plains overgrown with grasses. In these environments the birds are difficult to see, despite being fairly common and widespread, because their camouflage allows them to melt into the background.

Characteristics which can be used to differentiate between the two species are the thin black line which extends up the neck of the male black-bellied korhaan, and the white belly on the female black-bellied korhaan as opposed to the black belly of the female red-crested korhaan. During the spring mating season the males of the red-crested korhaan perform fascinating displays, often flying high into the sky then tumbling straight down for a considerable distance as though dead. Both species feed on any insects or small animals they can find, although the red-crested korhaan also has a distinct liking for plant fruits and seeds.

Despite its large size, the **Kori Bustard** *(Ardeotis kori)* is a close relative of dikkops and korhaans. The largest of the flying land birds, second in size only to the ostrich, this inconspicuous mottled brown and white bird is fairly common, but has a preference for the more open plains of the north. Here they slowly stalk about, in pairs or singly, feeding on insects, lizards, spiders, frogs, mice, bits of plant material and seeds.

DOVES

Doves are very common and several species occur in the area. The most abundant and widespread species are the **Cape Turtle Dove** *(Streptopelia capicola),* **Red-eyed Turtle Dove** *(S. semitorquata),* **Laughing Dove** *(S. senegalensis),* and the **Emerald-spotted Wood Dove** *(Turtur chalcospilos).* All four have a smoky-grey overall plumage. The Cape turtle dove and laughing dove become very tame in areas where contact with humans is frequent and left-over food from picnics is regular. In camps like Skukuza, Lower Sabie and Satara doves often walk boldly up to people lounging on a restaurant verandah and innocently peck at scraps and crumbs.

Although the emerald-spotted doves range throughout the Park, they tend to be rarer and more localized in their distribution. The twin bars across the back, and patch of green flecks on each wing make for easy recognition.

Doves are among the less energetic of home-makers. The nest consists of a simple platform of sticks almost haphazardly stuck together on a branch. Two eggs are normally laid in the nest and both parents will take turns to incubate and feed the young. Many doves use the same nest for successive breeding periods.

Some species, like the laughing dove, may form large flocks in areas where food is abundant. Here they will feed on small seeds and berries, occasionally taking an insect as well. Many such flocks can be seen in the open grass plains of the central area.

PARROTS

Used to caged parrots in domestic surroundings, my reaction when I first saw these birds flying wild and unfettered was of amazement and pleasant surprise. Most visitors probably share this feeling at their

Top left: Kori bustard (Photo: H. Jacobson) and (right) brown-headed parrot. Above: Laughing doves peck at crumbs in Pretoriuskop camp.

first such encounter. With a highly attractive covering of rich green feathers over the greater part of their bodies, these parrots have short tails and characteristic, curved and powerful bills. These are used to crack open seeds, to pulp fruit or berries, and to grip branches and twigs as a third 'foot' when clambering among trees in search of food. When breeding they nest in hollow branches, tree-trunks or logs, laying a clutch of four or more whitish eggs. During the day parrots can usually be seen flying or feeding in pairs or small groups.

There are two species of parrot in the Park. The **Brown-headed Parrot** *(Poicephalus cryptoxanthus)* is common and has a very wide distribution, generally announcing its presence by loud piercing shrieks. It is easily recognised by its all-brown head.

The **Brown-necked Parrot** *(P. robustus)* is less common and found only in the extreme north, around Punda Maria through to Pafuri. It is a larger species and adults have distinctive bright red patches on the head, shoulders and thighs. It prefers densely wooded areas or riverine forests, and has the same harsh call as the brown-headed parrot.

LOERIES

Medium-sized, but with long tails and prominent feathery crests on the head, loeries are widely distributed and fairly common. Two species occur in the Park.

The **Purple-crested Loerie** *(Tauraco porphyreolophus)* is extraordinarily beautiful with its contrasting shades of red, green and glossy purple. In flight the trailing edges of the wings are exposed to show a magnificent arc of scarlet feathers. In all it is one of the most handsome birds. Although often seen in drier, more open areas, they have a preference for tall trees on the edges of rivers or streams where, leaping from branch to branch, they search for fruit. They usually live in pairs, but are often seen alone. As their name implies, they have a stiff crest of purple feathers.

The uniformly coloured **Grey Loerie** *(Corythaixoides concolor)* is more drab in appearance, but has a charm all of its own. Its loud, almost mocking 'kwehhh' calls can be heard in all the fairly dry bushveld areas. More common than the purple-crested loeries, they are especially plentiful in the acacia woodland south of Tshokwane through to the Crocodile river. Normally found in small groups perched in the upper parts of trees, they live on fruits, flowers, insects and even small animals.

OWLS AND NIGHTJARS

Many species of owl contribute to the rich array of birds found in the Park. All are nocturnal predators which capture and feed on small creatures such as other birds, enormous numbers of mice, frogs, insects and sometimes even hares. An exception is the very rare **Fishing Owl** *(Scotopelia peli)* which scoops fish and crabs from the shallower waters of rivers. Several nests of these large and unusual birds have been found along the Luvuvhu river at Pafuri.

Most owls are mottled in patterns of brown, grey and black, and have a number of very useful adaptations to assist in their predatory way of life. Their senses of sight and hearing are exceptionally keen, enabling them to locate prey during twilight or in the reflected light of the moon, and among some species in total darkness, while modified wingfeathers enable them to swoop silently onto their prey. As they are only active at night they are rarely seen by visitors. With luck, an occasional individual may sometimes be seen during the day, perched in slumber in the branches of some tree.

Nightjars are much smaller than owls but are also nocturnal predators. All are mottled and speckled in varying shades of brown, with blotches of white helping to increase their camouflage. They have wide mouths, with short pointed beaks used to capture their insect prey. Several species are found, most of them being fairly common but rarely seen because of their nocturnal habits. Many sit on the ground in open clearings or on roads during the early hours of night, patiently waiting for insects to fly into view.

KINGFISHERS

The kingfishers form a fairly small but common group of birds, and several species are exceptionally beautiful with habits fascinating to watch.

The **Pied Kingfisher** *(Ceryle rudis)*,with a black collar around its neck and the remainder of its body bedecked with patterns of black and white, is common along all the rivers and larger streams. Mostly they are seen singly, sitting serenely on some branch along the river bank overlooking the water. Now and again they will fly low over the river surface for some distance and then suddenly swoop up and hover three or four metres above the water. Should a kingfisher see any fish of suitable size, it folds its wings and drops straight down, head first, into the water. A moment or two later it emerges with a small fish struggling in its beak. The bird carries the fish back to its perch, kills it by beating it against a branch, and then swallows it before repeating the whole cycle.

A bird with similar hunting habits is the **Giant Kingfisher** *(Ceryle maxima)*. It is the largest of the kingfishers and also has a predominantly black and white body. Giant kingfishers are fairly rare, but occur along all the major rivers.

Despite the misleading common name, there are several species of kingfishers which do not hunt fish and are not found near rivers at all.

The **Striped Kingfisher** *(Halcyon chelicuti)* occurs commonly throughout bushveld areas, generally perched quietly on a branch. Despite this nonchalant attitude it keeps a sharp lookout on the surrounding area, and every few minutes swoops from its perch to catch some insect blundering into view.

Left to right: Spiky footing for a grey loerie; Giant eagle owl shows its characteristic pink eyelids; and Woodland kingfisher.

Another common species often found in open bush, in summer, is the **Woodland Kingfisher** *(H. senegalensis),* its plumage shades of grey, black and blue. Like the striped kingfisher it swoops on insects in the vicinity and returns to its perch to kill and consume the prey.

Other species of kingfisher tend to be fairly rare and localized in their distribution. These include the half-collared kingfisher, malachite kingfisher, pygmy kingfisher, brown-hooded kingfisher and the grey-hooded kingfisher.

BEE-EATERS

Another group of highly attractive birds, the bee-eaters are bedecked with bright colours and have fairly long, sharply pointed bills. As their name suggests, they feed on bees but also devour a wide range of other insects. Perched on branches and logs, these gaily coloured birds will dart up and intercept any insect flying into view, gracefully gliding back to their perch to resume their vigil. Of the five species found in the Park, three are summer migrants.

The **Little Bee-eater** *(Merops pusillus)* and **White-fronted Bee-eater** *(M. bullockoides)* are widely distributed and common, nesting in burrows tunnelled into the side of earth banks such as those which have collapsed on the edges of rivers. As they live in colonies, large numbers of these holes are often seen together, white streaks from their accumulated droppings accentuating the entrances to the nests.

Of the three migratory species, the **Carmine Bee-eater** *(M. nubicoides)* is the most common, although the **European Bee-eater** *(M. apiaster)* also becomes abundant during mid-summer. Both these species are extremely beautiful and a great pleasure to watch.

White-fronted bee-eater (Photo: National Parks Board), and (right) lilac-breasted roller in the early-morning sun.

ROLLERS

These exquisitely coloured birds are a constant source of surprise and delight, their delicate hues of blue and pink blending with shades of other colours to produce an effect of riveting beauty.

There are five species of roller, all diurnal and much the same in general habits. They perch singly on prominent dead trees or projecting branches of a living tree, waiting quietly until some insect moves into view on the ground below. Then, with graceful acrobatic movements, they swoop to snatch the unsuspecting prey, and return to the perch to stun the prey by flicking it against the branch before swallowing it. Dedicated hunters, they are so intent on their task that all caution is thrown overboard when chasing their quarry. Very often, while concentrating on some insect crawling across the road, they will fly straight into the path of oncoming vehicles, and their lifeless bodies are often seen lying beside the road, especially in the northern half of the Park.

Of the five species the **Lilac-breasted Roller** *(Coracias caudata)* is the most common and widespread. It is more abundant in the open plains starting near Tshokwane in the south and stretching through to near Pafuri far in the north. The **European Roller** *(C. garrulus)* is a summer migrant, occasionally so abundant that it is even more commonly seen than the lilac-breasted roller.

All the rollers make their nests in holes in trees, laying up to three snowy-white eggs.

HORNBILLS

The **Yellow-billed** *(Tockus flavirostris)* and **Red-billed Hornbills** *(T. erythrorhynchus)* are common in the bushveld areas, both species often being found scratching in elephant-dung for beetles or other insects on which they feed. They also eat berries and seeds as well as any scraps of food left by visitors at picnic-sites or in the camps.

Hornbills have unusual nesting habits, the female being walled-in as a voluntary 'prisoner'. When the breeding season approaches, a tree with a suitable hole is selected and here the female remains whilst the male fetches a supply of mud. Together they seal off the entrance to the cavity, leaving only a small hole to connect the now-trapped female with the outside world. For several weeks the male feeds the female through this gap while she lays her eggs and later rears the young. Finally, when the young have grown sufficiently, the mud wall is broken down.

Several other species of hornbill are found, but these tend to be less common and have a more limited distribution. The **Grey Hornbills** *(T. nasutus)* and **Crowned Hornbills** *(T. alboterminatus australis)* have essentially similar habits to their more numerous relatives.

Somewhat larger and more striking are the **Trumpeter Hornbills** *(Bycanistes bucinator)*. Although their distribution stretches throughout the Park, they are common only in the riverine forest adjoining

Yellow-billed hornbill (left) and lesser striped swallow.

the Luvuvhu river at Pafuri. Normally found in groups, they have plaintive calls which closely resemble the forlorn sounds of a crying baby.

Ground Hornbills *(Bucorvus leadbeateri)* are the giants of this avian group. Throughout the Park these large, ponderous birds are found in groups of up to ten, usually seen strutting slowly along the road seeking insects or other small creatures such as frogs or lizards which make up their diet. If disturbed they swiftly take flight, but soon settle on a nearby tree. Like other hornbills they nest in cavities within trees, but do not seal the entrance holes.

SWALLOWS

Swallows are very common, especially during the summer months when they are often seen in flocks perched quietly on telephone wires along tarred roads, or rapidly swooping through the air seeking their insect prey.

Several species are found, some being permanent residents whilst others are temporary migrants from northern countries.

The **Lesser Striped Swallow** *(Hirundo abyssinica)* is fairly representative of the migratory species which breed in the Park during summer. This species occurs throughout the area, and is generally found in small groups at a particular locality. Like many other swallows, these build mud nests under overhanging rocks, under the eaves of roofs, and sometimes against trees – when no suitable rocks or ledges are available. The inside of the nest is lined with soft feathers, providing warmth and comfort for the chicks. Some swallow species tunnel into the soil of steep river banks to nest. Numerous such tunnels may be seen in suitable river banks, giving them a pock-marked appearance.

BULBULS

Predominantly brown with varied degrees of yellow markings, the bulbuls in the Park are all fairly small birds which feed on insects and fruit. They prefer well-wooded areas and make cup-shaped nests in the branches of trees or bushes, laying from two to four white eggs.

Of the five species which have been recorded, four are rare or have very localized distributions. Only the **Black-eyed Bulbul** *(Pycnonotus barbatus)* is widespread and common, being most abundant south of the Olifants river through to the Crocodile river. It is a very restless bird, rarely sitting quietly for any length of time, and prefers to bounce about the branches of fairly low trees, continuously investigating new areas. The black head and yellow patch at the base of the tail characterize this species, commonly seen perched in trees or on aloes in most of the camps.

HELMET SHRIKES

Fairly small, insectivorous birds, helmet shrikes have loosely arranged fluffy feathers on the front of the face, which droop partially over the bill. They live in small colonies, four to 20 strong, individual birds never venturing far from the group. Two species are found, widely distributed throughout woodland areas but avoiding the open grassy plains.

The **Red-billed Helmet Shrike** *(Prionops retzii)* has overall black plumage, white on the belly and tail. This contrasts strikingly with its red bill, legs, and a red circle around each eye.

The **White Helmet Shrike** *(P. plumata)* is more common and can be seen in all regions. Boldly marked in black and white, with yellow legs and eyes, these birds fly restlessly from bush to bush in small groups, often settling on the ground to search for insects.

Both species build comfortable, cup-shaped nests made of fine grasses and shredded vegetation, smoothed down with layers of silk collected from spider webs. The nests rest on branches in fairly low trees, generally containing three or four blotchy light green eggs.

Black-eyed bulbul (left) and white helmet shrike.

Top left: Glossy starling and (right) scarlet-chested sunbird. Above: Red-billed oxpeckers attending impala.

STARLINGS

Starlings are best known in the Park as noisy hordes of radiant purple birds so common in the southern parts. In fact, five species of these so-called glossy starlings are found, of which the **Cape Glossy Starling** *(Lamprotornis nitens)* is the most abundant and widespread. **Burchell's Glossy Starling** *(L. australis)* is also fairly common in the southern parts and is easily distinguished as it is larger than any of the other species and has a rather long, blunt-ended tail.

Numerous glossy starlings are usually seen at Tshokwane picnic-site and in Satara camp, their loud harsh voices often creating a terrific din.

As well as these purple-plumage species, three others are found, but are rather localised in their distribution. With black bodies and deep red wing feathers, the **Red-winged Starling** *(Onychognathus morio)* is rare and only found in certain rocky environments. The brownish **Wattled Starling** *(Creatophora cinerea)* is fairly common in open veld in the northern and central areas, while the very handsome **Plum-coloured Starling** *(Cinnyricinclus leucogaster)* is more common in the central and southern areas in summer.

Starlings feed on fruit and insects, although they happily scavenge left-over scraps of food in camps and picnic-sites. Most species nest in holes in trees, but the red-winged starlings prefer crevices in rocks or on rocky ledges. Wattled starlings build nests of sticks in thorny bushes, many hundreds often breeding together in the same small area.

OXPECKERS

Few will fail to notice these unusual birds, especially in the southern half of the Park. Usually found in small groups, oxpeckers prance about on the backs of a wide range of mammals, adeptly combing the coat in search of ticks, flies, and bits of dry skin. They are surprisingly well tolerated by most of their hosts, even being allowed to peer into the ticklish depths of an antelope's ears. Occasionally an animal may become irritated and flick a discouraging tail at the birds. They obligingly fly off, but soon return.

There are two species of oxpecker, both very similar in size and appearance. The **Yellow-billed Oxpecker** *(Buphagus africanus)* is extremely rare and unlikely to be seen. However, the **Red-billed Oxpecker** *(B. erythrorhynchus)* is widely distributed and common, most often seen on the backs of impala and giraffe. As most of the animals are found south of the Olifants river, it is understandable that these birds are similarly distributed.

SUNBIRDS

Petite little birds with long curving beaks, in the various species of this large group it is mostly the males which are brightly coloured in iridescent metallic sheens which glisten and sparkle in the sun. As nectar-feeders, their beautiful colours are further enhanced by the flowers they hover in front of or sit on. As well as nectar, they feed on small insects, thus ensuring a good supply of protein.

Sunbirds construct oval nests suspended from the ends of drooping branches, using grasses and fine strips of vegetation and occasionally rounding off the completed home with a plastering layer of silk raided from a spider's web. Two eggs are usually laid in each nest.

Of the many species which occur, the **Marico Sunbird** *(Nectarina mariquensis)* is the most widespread and abundant, males being strikingly adorned with feathers coloured in hues of green, red and black. The females are drab in comparison, bedecked in lustreless shades of brown. Both sexes are often seen cavorting around flowers in many of the camps.

A male lesser masked weaver puts the finishing touches to the entrance to a nest.

TRUE WEAVERS

Many species of weaver are found in the Park, some forming large swarms whose incessant chattering creates a terrific din. As their name implies, weavers construct nests of strips of plant material elaborately intertwined to form the most complex and elegant home built by any bird. The nest is used only once, so that each year the laborious building process must be repeated. Usually the nests are suspended from reeds or branches near rivers or pools of permanent water.

Among the Park's species are the spectacled weaver, red-headed weaver, spotted-backed weaver, Cape weaver, golden weaver and the masked weaver. Of these the **Spotted-backed Weaver** *(Ploceus cucullatus)* is probably the most abundant. They are common along all the main rivers and streams. Spotted-backed weavers, which feed on seeds and small insects, are usually seen in large flocks.

Although not always recognised as weavers by many visitors, there are other common or fairly common birds which belong to this group. These include the red-billed quelea, red bishop, Cape widow, golden bishop, white-winged widow, and the long-tailed widow. Most of these prefer open grassy veld and are common in the plains of the central area. Large flocks are often startled by approaching cars and take off *en masse* from the ground where they have been searching for seeds or small insects.

Reptiles

Unfortunately, man has always rather disdained, even disliked, the reptile world. Perhaps this is because of the scaly, stealthy and secretive appearance and habits of these creatures, as well as the poisonous nature of some. Nevertheless, reptiles are a very large and fascinating group with a very important position and rôle in the general web of life. They help substantially to maintain that delicate balance so critical for survival of all life. Secretive and quiet they may be, but they are largely responsible for containing the populations of small animals such as rats, mice and birds at a level which the environment can support. They help also to control the teeming millions of insects which so abundantly inhabit our planet. In turn, reptiles are preyed on by many species of birds and mammals.

Reptiles – including snakes, lizards, tortoises, terrapins and crocodiles – differ from birds and mammals in that they are unable to generate body heat internally, and thus maintain a temperature above that of their environment. Thus on cold days they are sluggish, and in colder countries they are forced to hibernate. This is why reptiles so often bask in the sun: to warm their bodies and speed up their metabolism. Unlike most amphibians, such as frogs, they are not restricted to water for breeding, but have evolved to a stage where they produce eggs covered by protective membranes and a shell which prevents the fragile embryo from drying out. The eggs are generally laid in the soil or on land, although some snakes and lizards retain the eggs within their bodies until they hatch, then give birth to live young.

In his excellent guide-book on the reptiles of the Kruger Park, Pienaar (1982) states that there are 114 different species occurring in the area, made up of 58 lizard species, 50 different snakes, five types of tortoises and terrapins, and a single crocodile species. Some of the more important or abundant species are:

SNAKES

Few people are neutral towards snakes. Feelings vary from the great love displayed by most snake-collectors to the more general fear and distaste, frequently bordering on revulsion. Ignorance and fallacy are often at the root of our distorted attitudes to these essentially shy and retiring creatures. Most snakes are not only harmless to man but actually assist us by helping to control potential rodent, bird and insect pests. Nevertheless, it is best to avoid snakes if you are not familiar with them nor certain of recognising the more dangerous species.

The **Black Mamba** *(Dendroaspis polylepis)* is perhaps the most feared and most notorious snake in southern Africa. Unlike its counterpart, the green mamba, which has never been found in the Park, it is widespread and common throughout the area. Despite the common name this mamba is never black, but generally greyish-brown above with a greyish-white belly. Adults more than four metres long have been recorded, but these were exceptional and a three-metre length is more common.

The black mamba is one of the few snakes which are instinctively aggressive and will not hesitate to strike. Nevertheless, when disturbed and if given the opportunity, it will prefer to retreat to its lair.

Although often seen lying curled up or lazily stretched along the branch of a tree, black mambas are more often encountered on the ground. They make their homes in abandoned termite nests, hollow tree-stumps, below rocks or logs, in old underground animal holes, or in the crevices and crannies of rocky outcrops. Unless disturbed, they will remain in the immediate vicinity of this home for many years, eating mice, birds and similar creatures.

Mamba venom is highly toxic and quick-acting. The poison attacks the nervous system causing respiratory failure and rapid death. Any snake resembling a mamba should be treated with respect.

Of the two species of cobra found throughout the Park, the largest – though never very common – is the **Egyptian** or **Banded Cobra** *(Naja haje annulifera),* with an average length of about two metres. They vary from yellowy-brown to browny-black above, with yellowy-brown undersides blotched in brown. A series of alternating light and dark bands mark the underside of the neck.

Generally, Egyptian cobras are not aggressive, preferring to move away from human presence. However, when suddenly disturbed they have the frightening habit of rearing up at great speed and spreading their necks in the characteristic hood to create a most menacing and formidable appearance. Unlike the Park's other cobra species, they do not spit venom and this display is essentially a fearsome show designed to frighten off the intruder and so prevent any further wasteful effort and energy. If further provoked, eventually they may bite, but more often prefer to roll over and sham death. Their venom is highly toxic and attacks the nervous system. The bite of an Egyptian cobra can result in a very quick death.

Their diet is widely varied, ranging from mice, birds, birds' eggs and frogs, even to other snakes and lizards. Like the black mamba, they make their homes in underground holes or below rocks, logs, in hollow tree-stumps or in termite hills.

The **Moçambique** or **Black-necked Spitting Cobra** *(Naja mossambica)* is fairly common and shows a distinct liking for old derelict buildings which probably attract food in the form of rats and mice. Generally about one metre long, this species is brown with yellowish undersides. A wide black bar with a series of narrower ones generally adorns the under-surface of the neck.

Black-necked spitting cobras are seen mostly at dusk or at night when they hunt mainly small animals such as mice, frogs, other reptiles, birds and their eggs, and occasionally some of the larger insects.

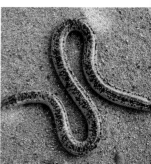

Left to right: African puff adder; Mole snake (Photo: Ian Espie); and Giant blind snake.

At such times they are rarely seen until one is very close when, invariably, they rear up with necks extended into a threatening hood. From this position they will stare the intruder straight in the eye for a considerable time, awaiting any sign of aggression. Any sudden move or advance in their direction is met by the cobra spitting venom – an incredibly fast squirt of poison directed at the eyes, and very accurate up to four or five metres. If poison does get into the eyes it causes immediate severe pain and may result in blindness if the venom is not thoroughly washed out fairly soon.

Like all snakes however, if unmolested, these adopt an attitude of live and let live towards humans, and because they are such effective predators of rodents, we do ourselves a dis-service by killing them.

The **African Puff Adder** *(Bitis arietans arietans)* is one of the snakes most frequently seen and is probably the most widespread and abundant species in Africa. Its upper skin varies from a light brown to a dark brown background superimposed on which are dark backward-pointing, arrow-head markings edged with a thin orange-yellow border. The large, triangular head has characteristic dark blotches, two above and one below each eye. Most puff adders are slightly less than a metre long, but have very fat bodies relative to their length, and short stumpy tails.

By day puff adders prefer somewhat dry bushveld areas, where they blend extremely well with their background earth and grass environment. Very sluggish by nature, they rely heavily on this camouflage to escape detection from natural predators such as secretary birds, eagles, ground hornbills and mongooses.

This reluctance to move, combined with their highly toxic venom, has earned them a reputation as one of the most feared snakes in Africa. Even when sensing approaching footsteps they will not move until they are actually stepped on. Then they retaliate with vicious suddenness, striking with incredible speed at the unsuspecting victim. The venom is relatively slow-acting, but causes breakdown of the blood cells and severe bleeding accompanied by large-scale swelling and intense pain, and results in death unless treatment is received.

113

Puff adders hunt at night, preying on small animals such as rats and mice, birds, frogs and lizards. They are very sensitive to cold and soon hibernate with the approach of winter.

The four preceding species constitute the most dangerous of the poisonous snakes occurring in the Park. Other venomous snakes, like the **Tree-snake** or **Boomslang** *(Dispholidus typus)*, **Southern Vine** or **Twig-snake** *(Thelotornis capensis)*, **Shield-nosed Snake** *(Aspidelaps scutatus)* and the **Snouted Night-adder***(Causus defilippii)* are rather less common and certainly seldom seen. They are also less dangerous, and on the whole reluctant to bite.

There is also a very wide range of non-poisonous species, the best-known of which is, without doubt, the **African Python** *(Python sebae natalensis)*. It is the largest of the African snakes, often reaching five to six metres in length, although generally between four and five metres long. Because of their considerable girth, they present a rather frightening appearance when suddenly seen at close quarters. Black-edged, irregular-shaped dark brown blotches on a light brown background colour the upper surface of the snake, whilst the underside is yellowish-white. The blotchings break up the shape of the python, providing excellent camouflage and allowing it to remain undetected in shrubby riverine or bushveld undergrowth. Very sluggish by nature, pythons prefer to let their prey walk right up to them before lunging to encircle the quarry in their sinewy and highly muscular coils. Although they have no poison, they will bite without hesitation if provoked, sinking a discouraging array of sharpened backward-directed teeth into their victim. Pythons kill their prey – normally small animals such as mice, birds, rabbits and even young antelope – by suffocating them with their constricting coils and then swallowing them whole. Body components which cannot be digested, such as bones and horns, are regurgitated after the soft tissues have been absorbed. If they are threatened and cannot escape fast enough due to the weight of their prey, pythons will often disgorge whole animals.

Fairly common through the area, they are generally spotted when basking in the sun in an open patch of veld or crossing roads.

Other harmless snakes commonly found are the **Brown House Snake** *(Lamprophis fuliginosus)*, **Cape Wolf-snake** *(Lycophidion capense)*, **Green** or **Spotted Bush-snake** *(Philothamnus semivariegatus)*, **Common Green Water-snake** *(Philothammus hoplogaster)*, **Common Egg-eater** *(Dasypeltis scabra)*, and the **Southern Stripe-bellied Sand-snake** *(Psammophis subtaeniatus subtaeniatus)*.

The chances of a visitor to the Park being bitten by a snake are extremely slim. Nevertheless, should this unlikely event occur, CONTACT THE NEAREST GAME-RANGER or CAMP-MANAGER AS SOON AS POSSIBLE. Even if you have been bitten, DON'T PANIC – the chances are that it was probably by some harmless species. If you suspect a mamba bite, immediately tie a tourniquet around the affected limb ABOVE the bite. If bitten by any other species, do not apply a tourniquet: you will do more damage than good.

114

LIZARDS

Lizards, in a wide range of sizes and colours, are found anywhere and everywhere in the Park. They live under and on the ground, in trees, in houses, even in rivers and dams. They are the creatures that scuttle away so rapidly to crevices and cracks at the first approach of humans, but soon cannot resist peeking out to cast curious and fascinated glances at these animals called people. We miss such a wonderful little world by ignoring these seemingly minor denizens of the bush, so busily engaged in the tiresome business of survival – our evolutionary predecessors that can be so informative and pleasing to observe.

Most lizards feed almost exclusively on insects, and as this prey is so abundant and occurs in such a wide range of habitats, it is understandable that lizards are numerous and widespread. They are highly effective predators of insects and form one of the most efficient groups of animals which help prevent insects from becoming over-abundant. Watch how expertly the **Common Dwarf Gecko** *(Lygodactylus capensis capensis)* stalks and catches moths or other insects which venture within striking distance of this seemingly harmless little reptile.

Dwarf geckos are abundant and are commonly seen resting on walls or fence-posts in all the rest-camps. One of the smallest lizards, a fully grown adult is only about 70 to 80 millimetres long. Generally light grey, these geckos have a pale streak, bordered above and below with a dark edge running on either side of the body from the snout to the hind-legs. Some individuals are very dark however, being more brown than grey.

Another species often seen on the walls of buildings in the Park is the **Tropical** or **House Gecko** *(Hemidactylus mabouia)*. These are also mainly insectivorous and can be seen at night feeding on moths or other insects which collect around lights in the various camps. Full-grown they average about 120 millimetres in length, having a

A tree agama shows its excellent camouflage, and (right) common East African chameleon.

mottled greyish body, irregularly patterned with brown or blackish blobs. In the bush they blend very well with the general background colour of the bark of the trees. They also live among scattered hillside rocks, sharing this habitat with a range of other species.

Perhaps more familiar because of its size and habits, is the **Tree** or **Black-necked Agama** *(Agama atricollis)*. Between 160 and 210 millimetres long, these lizards are commonly seen scuttling around the trunks of trees, especially acacias. Why acacia trees are preferred is uncertain, though it may be connected with the types of insects found in them, or it may be that acacias coincidentally prefer the type of general environment, such as soil and climate, in which tree agamas thrive. Certainly the colour and texture of acacia bark provides excellent camouflage and foothold for these lizards, which nimbly run along the branches, totally defying gravity. Their coloration is best described as a jumble and mixture of various shades of grey and brown, which they combine to create a highly effective camouflage, particularly when seen against such trees as the knobthorn *(Acacia nigrescens)*.

In summer, during the breeding season, many males become brightly garbed to attract female attention. Shades of blue adorn the back and other parts of the body, the top of the head becomes coppery-green, certain parts of the body display orangey-yellow marks, and the tail changes to a dull green or olive-brown. The total effect is a very handsome lizard indeed. As the mating season recedes and winter approaches, these colours become increasingly dull until they fade to the usual overall grey.

To me, the most unusual and most interesting of the local lizards is the **Common East African** or **Flap-necked Chameleon** *(Chamaeleo dilepis dilepis)*, the only species of chameleon found in the Park. Common and widespread throughout the area, it is a true lizard, though most people subconsciously tend to place this creature in a

A water leguaan (left) and a young tree leguaan.

116

separate category, thinking of 'lizards' and 'chameleons' rather than lumping them in one group as they should. This differentiation has three main reasons: a chameleon's sluggish habits, its ability to change colour, and its facility of moving each eye independently.

Most lizards depend on speed and agility to capture their prey and escape their enemies and this is reflected in their long, streamlined bodies. Chameleons have adopted an alternate strategy, and their robust, squat body is one result of this.

Rather than expend energy on scurrying about to secure prey or slip from the clutches of the enemy, they slowed right down, creeping stealthily and ever so slowly to within striking distance of a tasty insect, at the last moment flicking out a long, muscular tongue which sticks to the prey and instantly recurls bearing the food to the mouth. To avoid detection from other predators, chameleons have developed the remarkable ability to change colour, so that they blend with and seem part of their background. They also have the ability, unique in the animal world, to move and focus each eye on a separate point. Often one eye looks forward to see where it is going, whilst the other eye is trained on some point behind.

When threatened, chameleons become very dark of body and inflate themselves to appear bigger, as well as extending the yellowy-orange pouch below the head. If further disturbed, they hiss to increase the defence display, their open mouths showing the red insides. The combined effect of colour changes and posturing is surprisingly effective and usually frightens off the intruder. Even people who know chameleons to be absolutely harmless will refrain from picking them up when they exhibit these threat displays, simply because they appear so very aggressive.

The two species of leguaan found in the Park are by far its largest lizards. The widespread **Rock** or **Tree Leguaan** *(Varanus exanthematicus albigularis)* grows to about 1,3 metres in length and, despite its size and deceptively slow gait under normal circumstances, is capable of running at considerable speed when threatened or disturbed. Appropriate to their large size, however, tree leguaans often will retaliate and behave aggressively. Then they lift themselves off the ground, hiss loudly, lash out with their tails if the intruder ventures too close, and bite furiously at any nearby object.

The tree leguaan is an overall greyish-brown, with light and dark shades blotching the body in various patterns, a coloration affording excellent camouflage in its natural environment of rocky hills or boulder-strewn bushveld. Though they prefer being on firm ground, these leguaans can climb trees with ease when necessary. Unlike the smaller lizards which are mainly insectivorous, the tree leguaan feeds on mice, birds, other lizards, snakes, and any eggs it can find. In turn, it is preyed on by such mammals as the smaller cats and honey badgers, as well as many raptors.

A close relative, the **Water** or **River Leguaan** *(Varanus niloticus)* prefers living in and around permanent sources of water such as rivers and dams. They are about two metres long and in coloration differ from the tree leguaan in having small yellowy markings dotted on a greyish-brown body, broken further by greenish-yellow bands here and there. Common along all the major rivers, they are often seen basking in the sun on some rock or fallen log beside the water. However, they are very shy and will dive into the water at the first sign of disturbance, swimming submerged for some distance before reappearing. They swim strongly and are obviously well adapted to their watery environment, in keeping with which they feed mainly on small fish, crabs and mussels, though they happily add birds' eggs to their diet.

Other species of lizard, many exceedingly beautiful in colour, are abundant on the hills, plains and riversides. Rocky hills, which provide easily-found homes in the numerous crevices, especially attract large numbers of lizards. Vegetation growing between the stones attracts insects, so providing a source of food, and the rock gardens in many of the camps usually have enough lizards to provide visitors with pleasure and entertainment during those leisurely hours in camp.

CROCODILES

Of the 25 surviving species of the crocodile family, only the **Nile Crocodile** *(Crocodylus niloticus)* occurs in the Park, where it is common in all the major rivers – a very successful inhabitant which poses a constant threat to animals seeking a life-sustaining sip of water.

Visitors often ask about the colour differences between individual crocodiles. The colour varies according to the creature's age, young crocodiles being light brown or yellowish-green; with advancing age, this darkens, until old specimens are dark grey or almost black on top. The underside of a crocodile remains pale throughout life.

Adult crocodiles in the Park average about four metres in length, and older specimens sometimes become very obese. At close quarters, their elongate mandibles lined with a mutilating row of vicious teeth, combined with an unflinching, cold emotionless stare, present the appearance of a merciless and fearless killer. And so they are. Not cruel, but nevertheless a calmly calculating, highly effective instrument of death which kills to survive. Even today the crocodile is responsible for more human deaths in Africa than any other large animal. In the Park, several people have lost their lives to these reptiles, in each case due to foolhardy self-confidence and disregard for the potent capability and competence of these silent monsters which lurk and reign supreme in their watery world.

During daylight crocodiles are often seen lying on rocks or sandbanks, contentedly absorbing the warming rays of the sun. Sometimes they lie with their mouths agape, apparently an adaptation which helps heat exchange between the body and outside environment through the thin membranes of the mouth. At other times they can be

Reflected sun glistens on two Nile crocodiles.

seen slowly cruising just below the surface, with only their eyes and nostrils above water. Like those of the hippopotamus, their eyes and nostrils are situated on raised extensions elevated above the general level of the head so that they can still see and breathe while the remainder of the body is submerged.

Crocodiles prefer to catch prey when these come down to the river to drink. Carefully observing the animal as it stoops for water, the crocodile slowly approaches underwater, at the last moment grabbing the unfortunate victim by the snout. Any animal which ventures within striking range is likely to be taken; even buffalo and giraffe fall prey to crocodiles. With frightful splashing and great commotion the animal is dragged under water and held, its struggles becoming more and more feeble, until it drowns. If the prey is large and thick-skinned it is allowed to rot, and so become easier to rip apart before it is devoured. Younger crocodiles which cannot overcome medium- and large-sized mammals have to be content with a diet of fish, crabs, mussels, frogs or anything small and meaty which comes their way.

Crocodiles lay their eggs below the soil, digging a hole in a sandbank or soft earth adjoining the river. The eggs are deposited in layers, each of which is covered with a protective blanket of sand or soil. Though the female spends a great deal of time guarding this nest, many crocodile eggs are dug up and eaten by other animals such as leguaans, otters, water mongooses, even marabou storks. When the young are ready to hatch they make a squeaky sound. This warns the mother, who removes the sandy covering while the youngsters break open their shells using a temporary tooth on the tip of the snout. This horny 'tooth' falls off soon after serving its purpose.

A mating pair of leopard tortoises.

TORTOISES AND TERRAPINS

Reptiles have a long evolutionary history which goes back more than 150 million years. But whereas most other reptiles became elongate and streamlined, tortoises and terrapins followed a different survival strategy. The body shortened and became broader, which tends to slow down the animal. Slow animals always have problems of self-protection, so to prevent themselves being too vulnerable to predators, these reptiles evolved a shell into which they could withdraw when threatened. The success of this adaptation is apparent from their survival over all these millions of years, and today they still thrive in most parts of the globe.

Two species of tortoise and three of terrapin occur in the Park.

The **Leopard** or **Mountain Tortoise** *(Geochelone pardalis babcocki)* is the species most often seen on land anywhere in the area. Specimens half a metre long and with a mass of more than 25 kilograms have been recorded, although such large individuals are unlikely to be found under conditions in the Park where they would fall prey to some animal before reaching an advanced size. The shell is rounded above and brightly patterned with irregular yellow and black markings, from which the name 'leopard' tortoise probably derives. Vegetarians, they feed on the leaves of a wide range of plants including the more tasty grasses, and sometimes even on fungi. Despite the protective armour of the shell, large numbers of tortoises are killed every year by such animals as hyenas, mongooses, as well as by ground hornbills and other predatory birds. Mating takes place in spring and early summer, after which the female digs a hole in soft soil and lays six or so round, white eggs. These are covered over and may take more than a year to hatch, by which time the female has long since departed for better pastures and the youngsters must fend for themselves.

The **Hinged-back Tortoise** *(Kinixys belliana spekii),* the other terrestrial species, is fairly rare and only occurs in the western half of the

120

Hinged-back tortoise (left) and hinged terrapin.

Park. Much the same as the leopard tortoise in general habits, it differs in appearance. The shell is flattened on top, giving the tortoise a flatter and elongate, rather than rounded, appearance. A drab greeny-brown, these tortoises reach only about 180 millimetres in length. Many are killed each year by animal predators and by veld fires.

Often seen sitting on rocks or logs which protrude from the river surface, the **Hinged Terrapin** *(Pelusios sinuatus)* lives in water and is found in all the major rivers and permanent waterholes. It has a uniform grey-black body, flattened from top to bottom. This flattened shape decreases water resistance, streamlining it for better forward propulsion. Adults reach a maximum length of about 300 millimetres.

Like its Cape relative, the hinged terrapin is carnivorous, feeding on a wide range of small water creatures such as frogs, tadpoles, fish, crabs and insect larvae. Given the opportunity, they will also scavenge bits of flesh from the prey of crocodiles. These, their main enemies, catch and eat large numbers of terrapins.

The **Cape Terrapin** *(Pelomedusa subrufa)* is slightly smaller and even more flattened than the hinged terrapin. Although much the same in colour, it can be recognized by this very flat appearance and lack of the slightly elevated knobs which run down the shell on the back of the hinged terrapin. The Cape terrapin is rare and only found in some of the temporary pools and dams. When these dry up in the drier winter months, each terrapin buries itself in the muddy bottom, peacefully hibernating in its protective tomb until the spring rains fall.

As does the hinged terrapin, this species spends long periods underwater but is forced to surface once in a while for air. At other times it basks on some rock or at the water's edge, or searches for a snack of crab, fish, snail, insect or other small meaty morsel.

The rare **Pan Hinged Terrapin** *(Pelusios subniger)* has recently been discovered in temporary pans in the Nyandu sandveld, south of Pafuri.

Frogs

On the evolutionary scale, frogs fall between fishes and reptiles – they are more advanced than fish, but less developed than reptiles.

The first living organisms on our earth started life in the sea, they lived and died there, and countless millions of generations remained bound to this marine existence. But life has a marvellous way of adapting itself to better survive in its particular environment. So it was that, during the course of these millions of generations, there would arise every so often a single individual which, by genetic accident, was slightly better suited to a given environment than its companions. Many of these individuals died, but enough survived and reproduced for their beneficial characters to persist in the community – resulting in increasingly complex organisms which could better withstand the rigours of the environment. In this way single-cell organisms, which had no control over themselves and drifted helplessly with wind and current, evolved into fishes which could swim about seeking food and shelter, so increasing their own chances of survival.

Some of these fish started living in the estuaries of rivers; of these some became more adept at surviving in fresh water; and in time fish evolved which swam and lived successfully in inland rivers. Many of these rivers dry up during part of each year, forming pools of stagnant water poor in oxygen content. It was in such pools, where they could no longer rely on their gills to provide them with oxygen, that fish developed lungs which they used to gulp air at the surface.

But often the pools could not provide them with food so – again through a series of genetic accidents and over many generations – some fish slowly lost their fins, these becoming more limb-like, until a fish-like organism with crude legs evolved, which could periodically move out of water to search for food on land. From these organisms the frogs developed, and even today they spend part or all of their lives in water.

Most frogs cannot lay eggs that survive on dry land. Unlike reptiles or birds, their eggs have no shell to prevent them drying out or being damaged. Because of this they have to lay their eggs in water, whether in rivers, streams, or even small temporary pools left by rain. These eggs become tadpoles, which are just like fish in that they have gills and a fin-like broadened tail to aid swimming. As the tadpoles grow older and larger they develop lungs, the tail becomes shorter, and legs start growing from the creatures' sides. They become more and more dependant on their lungs, relying less on their gills which become smaller and eventually disappear. A few species of frog, such as the platanna, remain in water all their lives, but the vast majority leave their watery nursery to become true denizens of the land, returning to water only to lay their eggs and so continue the cycle.

There are 33 species of frog in the Park, many so abundant that it would be accurate to say that it is the home of more frogs than of birds or mammals. Only because frogs are fairly small, so well camouflaged, attract little attention and are mostly active at night, do we underestimate their abundance and even their importance. Frogs are a crucial part of the Park's web of life, eating huge numbers of insects, including mosquito larvae, and themselves forming a source of food for many reptiles, birds and mammals.

Two species of frog in the area live permanently in water except for short periods when they may migrate from one pool to another: the **Common Platanna** *(Xenopus laevis laevis)* and the **Northern Platanna** *(Xenopus muelleri)*. Despite its name, the common platanna has only been found in certain pools and pans around Pretoriuskop, whereas the northern platanna is widespread in most situations where there is quiet or stagnant water, such as in dams, pans, or the backwater pools of the main rivers. Both species are similar in general appearance and habits. They are flat and broad, with their eyes on top of the head so they can see upwards when lying on the pool bottom. They vary from greenish-grey to charcoal-black above, with pale grey to white or yellowy undersides. The northern platanna is slightly smaller, reaching only about 70 millimetres in length, and has a characteristic short tentacle below each eye.

Using their thick and strong hindlegs, they pounce and feed on small animals which share their home, such as the tadpoles of other frog species or small fish which may venture within range. The large hind feet are webbed, enabling frogs to swim very swiftly, kicking out

A red-banded frog during a summer shower.

The foam nest of a grey tree frog overhangs a temporary pool near Punda Maria. Top right: Red toad, and olive toad (right).

with their legs and displacing large amounts of water. Their eggs are surrounded by a jelly-like substance which protects and holds them to such underwater sites as stones or vegetation.

Grass-frogs of the genus *Ptychadena* are very common along the grass- or weed-covered edges of rivers, streams, pools or dams. They are roughly triangular in shape, broad at the hind-end but tapering sharply to the snout, to give an agile and streamlined appearance, as indeed they are. Using their powerful hindlegs they can jump large distances, executing a series of leaps to reach the water and escape any source of disturbance.

Between 40 and 60 millimetres long when full-grown, their bodies are usually reddish-brown and marked with blotches or bands, depending on the species. In the evenings during spring and summer, especially after rain has fallen, the mating calls of these frogs combine with those of other frogs in an almost deafening orchestration of multi-pitched sounds which herald a frenzied search for mates so that eggs can be laid in the fresh supply of water. With the coming of winter these frogs hibernate in the cracks of dried-out pans or in crevices and holes of nearby logs and trees.

One of the more unusual frogs to be seen is the **Grey Tree Frog** *(Chiromantis xerampelina)*. This fairly large, grey species which inhabits trees, occurs commonly throughout the area. Their long, thin legs, unlike the highly muscular hindlegs of most other frogs, are adapted for clambering about on branches, where their colour blends well with that of the bark. The toes and fingers have sucker-like discs which help them cling to smooth surfaces.

In spring and summer they congregate around pools, laying their eggs in frothy masses which hang suspended from branches or other vegetation drooping over the pool. Initially the female deposits a liquid which, with their legs, she and the male vigorously churn and whip into the characteristic white frothy mass. The froth protects the eggs it contains, not only hiding them from view but also keeping them moist. After hatching, the young tadpoles wriggle inside this froth for a few days, then drop to the water to continue their search for food, and progress to adulthood.

One of the very few frogs which have managed to eliminate the need for pools of water is the **Common Blaasop** *(Breviceps mossambicus adspersus)*. It grows to about 60 millimetres, the males being smaller than females. Found throughout the Park, especially where the soil is rather sandy, these are burrowing frogs with a rounded, bloated body which is yellowy-orange, banded and mottled with dark brown. The legs, which seem short and stubby compared with the obese body, are a good adaptation for an underground way of life – long, gangling limbs would be an impediment to any burrower. Like those of moles, their hands and feet are modified as digging organs.

The common blaasops spend the greater part of their lives underground, feeding on soil-dwelling insects such as termites, ants, or beetle larvae. They emerge only when rains flood the soil or when searching for mates. During mating the male becomes literally 'glued' to the back of the female by a sticky substance. The jelly-covered eggs are laid in a neatly dug underground hole. After hatching, the young, which resemble normal tadpoles, have to fend for themselves by wriggling about in search of food.

Six species of toad of the genus *Bufo* occur. These are the frogs most often noticed, not only because they are fairly large and some of the species are abundant, but also because they jump around in the open veld hunting insects or other small prey. All of them have a rough and bumpy skin, are very similar in shape, and tend to be brown with various blotches or markings to aid their camouflage.

The most common and most widespread of these is the **Olive Toad** *(Bufo garmani)*. It grows to just less than 100 millimetres, and a series of bold but attractive reddish block-patterns adorns its yellowy-brown body. In spring and summer, especially after rains, their loud and throaty croaks are a very common sound in the vicinity of pools and pans. Numerous eggs are laid in these pools, where the tadpoles provide a great source of food to fish or other aquatic predators.

An excellent book by Pienaar, Passmore and Carruthers (1976), *The Frogs of the Kruger National Park,* is available at most restcamps. It describes in detail each of the frogs, and colour illustrations make it easy to identify the various species.

Fishes

Under the rippled surfaces of the permanent rivers or in the murky depths of the numerous dams and pools, a teeming multitude of, literally, millions of fish form yet another link in the imposing array of wildlife forms which make up the web of life in the Park. Unseen by most visitors, 49 species of fish share their aquatic home with hippos, crocodiles, terrapins, and numerous invertebrates. Though we tend to underestimate the importance of these fish, they too contribute to the Park's cycle, feeding on each other, on crabs, snails, countless insects, small water-plants, and in turn serving as food for a large variety of birds and mammals.

Many of the species are well known, such as the streamlined aristocrat of the freshwater environment, the tigerfish *(Hydrocynus vittatus)*, often caught by anglers outside the Park. Highly agile predators, these excellent game-fish are summer migrants to the Park, returning to the Moçambique lowlands during winter to spawn.

Other well-known fish include the large-scaled yellowfish *(Barbus marequensis)*, several species of labeo or mudfish *(Labeo* spp.), a range of tilapia or kurper *(Tilapia* spp.), and the very common sharptooth catfish *(Clarias gariepinus)*. Frequently reaching a mass between 10 and 25 kilograms, this opportunistic catfish is an omnivorous scavenger or predator preferring the quiet waters of dams and pans, or the slow backwaters of rivers. During floods, large numbers of catfish of-

A tiger fish caught in Luvuvhu river.

Catfish dying in the muddied remains of a temporary pool.

ten collect in the pools which form along rivers. As the waters recede the pools slowly shrink under the hot sun, and eventually hundreds of these extraordinarily tough fish can be seen slowly gasping to death, their tangled bodies twitching as the last survivors struggle desperately through the mud for air. One of Nature's methods of population control, this also feeds a hungry horde of scavenging birds and mammals that feast on the unexpected food supply.

Without doubt the most beautiful, and perhaps the most unusual, of the many species of small fish to be found in the Park, are the two species of killifish *(Notobranchius orthonotus* and *N. rachovii)*. Brilliantly coloured in hues of red, green and blue, these fish live in temporary pools which dry completely during summer. The adult fish die, but their eggs lie buried in the surface layers of mud, ready to hatch when the rains of the following season return the pool to a life-sustaining habitat once more. More details of these and other fascinating fish are provided in the well-illustrated guide-book by Pienaar (1978) on the *Freshwater Fishes of the Kruger National Park.*

Scorpions, spiders and other Arthropods

All these groups of small creatures – together with insects, ticks, mites, crustacea and a few others – share certain characteristics which make them close relatives of each other and allow them to be grouped together as the Arthropoda. The arthropods are so numerous that they comprise about four-fifths of some 1,25 million animal species known to man. Most of these are insects, which are described in a later section.

All these arthropods have several pairs of jointed legs arranged along the sides of the body. Another shared character is that they have a tough skin, or cuticle, made up of a substance called chitin. Unlike humans, who have an internal bony framework, these animals have a fairly rigid skin as a skeleton to which all the muscles are attached. The skin also protects them against the hot, drying rays of the sun, allowing them to move into the open to hunt and search for mates.

SCORPIONS

Few animals on earth evoke such instant human fear and revulsion as do scorpions. Yet, as with most other dangerous or poisonous creatures, they are aggressive towards us only if we threaten their lives or disturb their activities. Left alone they will live and grow, feed and reproduce, spending most of the day resting in some protected crack, crevice or hole, emerging only at night to forage.

Scorpions have six pairs of jointed limbs. The front pair is small and modified to serve as jaws, called chelicerae. The second pair is very large and has become modified as claws or pincers, known as pedipalps. The remaining four pairs are typical legs used for walking and running.

Africa is home to a surprisingly large number of scorpion species, many of which are found in the Park. These range in length from about 20 millimetres to giants measuring 180 millimetres from mouth to tail tip.

Most species of scorpion fall within two families, fairly easy to recognize. The Scorpionidae have slender tails but powerful, thick claws on the second pair of limbs. The sting at the end of the tail can be painful but they depend mainly on their claws to capture and hold their prey – insects, spiders or other small creatures. By contrast, the Buthidae have thick tails but small claws. The venom in their sting is highly poisonous and is used to kill or paralyse their prey, the claws then being used to carry or manipulate the food. Several species of these thick-tailed scorpions occur but are seen only rarely because of their shy and secretive habits.

A vicious struggle ends as a poisonous scorpion defeats a solifuge.

Largest of the scorpions in the Park belong to the group *Hadogenes* and live in the cracks and crevices of rocky outcrops where they are amazingly adept at moving on and clinging to almost vertical rock surfaces. They have very flattened bodies which allow them to crawl into narrow openings.

Members of the group *Uroplectes* are common and generally found under logs or beneath the peeling bark of trees. Most are about 40 to 50 millimetres long, with orange-brown or dark green bodies. They are especially common in the northern areas around Punda Maria and Pafuri, and occasionally are seen in the evenings scuttling about on logs or fence-posts. Species of the group *Opisthancanthus* also live below the bark of trees throughout the Park, but are somewhat larger and darker than *Uroplectes*. Whereas *Uroplectes* have thick tails, indicating that they are poisonous, *Opisthancanthus* have slender tails.

Many members of the group *Parabuthus* excavate narrow tunnels going down for as much as a metre into the earth. These are the rogues of the scorpion-world, small-clawed but with massive tails which they lift menacingly toward any potential enemy. Grey-black, they strut about in silent arrogance in the instinctive knowledge that few animals will dare to tamper with them. Several people have died after being stung by these scorpions. The pain brought on by their poison is excruciating and anti-venom should be administered quickly to victims of their stings. Although fairly common, *Parabuthus* scorpions are fortunately not a problem as they tend to shun areas where humans live.

Scorpions are unable to control their body temperatures as mammals and birds do, so that when winter's cold approaches they become more and more reluctant to venture out into the open. With all their body activities slowed down, they snuggle into some crevice or hole and wait for the warmth of spring. Only then do they emerge to search for insects or other prey to replenish their famished bodies. This emergence also signals a search for mates, though copulation does not take place. Instead the male drops a packet of sperm on the ground, grabs the female's pincers or claws in his own, and then directs her towards the immortalizing sperm. Once she has been guided onto the sperm, the female positions herself and depresses her body so that the sperm is taken up.

Young scorpions are born alive, and crawl onto the back of the female for protection.

SPIDERS

Like insects, spiders are numerous and widespread, occurring all around us, in and on the soil, on and under rocks and logs, under tree-bark and on leaves and flowers, in our houses, and even in water. They have an amazing range of habits and vary greatly in appearance. When full-grown they may measure less than a millimetre or become hairy gargantuans 150 millimetres or more in length. And yet, as with the insects, we live in almost total ignorance of these fascinating micro-inhabitants which help make our earth acceptable to us as humans by keeping insect numbers down to an acceptable level. Millions of insects are trapped each day in the sinewy strands of spider-webs; in return, spiders are consumed in vast quantities by beetles, wasps or other insects. Baboons, mice, birds, snakes, lizards and many other animals find part of their daily sustenance among the multitude of spiders which scurry and scuttle in the vegetation, or wait with endless patience at their little homespun webs.

Like scorpions, spiders have six pairs of jointed limbs. The first pair is modified as jaws or fangs, the second pair has been adapted to serve as feelers, and the remaining four pairs function as legs.

Their bodies are divided into two parts – a small front section which contains the eyes, mouth and legs, and a larger hind-part which houses the intestines and silk-producing organs. The silk is extruded from tiny pores near the rear of the body, either as thin individual strands or broad collective sheets. Many small spiders will use their silk as a means of 'flying'. Clinging to the upper part of a grass-blade or projecting piece of vegetation, they stream out a thin strand of silk which is caught by any faint breath of wind. When the strand is long enough and the breeze sufficiently strong, the spider releases its grip and, aided by the silken streamer, drifts with the wind until eventually caught up in vegetation elsewhere. Early on a summer's morning one can often see literally thousands of these strands strewn haphazardly across a dirt road – visible when the sun reflects off the silk at the correct angle.

The silk is mainly used to build webs, to line the walls of tunnel-building species, or to wrap the spider's prey in an envelope of silk.

Gasteracantha spider (left) and orb-spinning *Nephila.*

One of the most beautiful of bushveld sights is a dew-laden web with sparkling drops reflecting crystal shafts of morning light. It is in such unexpected, unasked for moments when Nature briefly reveals her finest gems, that awake a deep and lasting appreciation of the simple but boundless beauty of the smaller organisms which live unnoticed all around us.

Numerous species of spider occur in great abundance throughout the Park. Most are small and shy, tucked away in shrouding masses of vegetation where they remain undetected by human eyes. Others, seen more often, venture into camps where they crawl on the walls of huts or sit patiently outdoors on flowers or leaves. But those which attract the most attention are the large, multicoloured orb-spinners of the genus *Nephila,* whose massive golden webs are strung between adjacent trees. The webs of tough and very thick strands attract as much attention as the beautifully coloured spiders themselves. The female has a body length of about 20 millimetres but her long dangling legs make her appear much larger. The male is very much smaller – sometimes with a mass only one-thousandth that of the female. She constructs the large web and occupies the prime position. The males must be content with staying on the fringes of the web, feeding on offal or tiny insects disdained by the female. Only when she is busily engaged in consuming a tasty grasshopper or similar insect will a male cautiously approach and clamber onto the female to attempt mating. During mating she ignores the male, continues to feed, seemingly unaware of the reproductive act. Many female spiders catch and consume the male soon after mating, his protein adding to the nutrients which help feed the new life already beginning to stir inside her.

Another large spider which slings conspicuous webs between vegetation is the somewhat flattened *Argiope* sp., the long legs pleasantly patterned in alternate light and dark bands. Unlike *Nephila* which have elongate bodies, these spiders have a rounded overall shape.

Spiders of the genus *Gasteracantha* are somewhat smaller than *Nephila* or *Argiope,* but also build webs which are suspended between

131

branches of trees. Although only about 10 millimetres long, these spiders catch the eye because of the spiky growths projecting from the sides of their bodies. The legs are very short and the upper surface of the body is brilliantly coloured with bold shades of red or yellow.

As well as these web-building species, there is a multitude of other spiders which do not depend on their silk to catch their prey. Some sit quietly on the soil or bits of vegetation, deceptively calm and apparently at peace with the world, then pounce with terrifying suddenness on any small insect which stumbles into view. Others again, like the massive hairy baboon spiders, sacrifice all caution and boldly hunt down their victims. So called because their dense coat of dark hairs is somewhat reminiscent of that of a baboon, these spiders drive deep tunnels into the soil. Lined with silk, these are their retreats where they can rest and care for their young. Most of the large spiders which hunt for prey belong to the genera *Harpactirella*, *Pterinochilus*, and *Ceratogyrus*. They are active at night and have strong thick legs radiating from huge, dark-coloured bodies which, when full-grown, tend to vary between 40 and 50 millimetres long.

'SUN SPIDERS' OR SOLIFUGES

Despite a superficial resemblance to spiders, solifuges are a totally different group, with their own unique structures and adaptations. Though fairly common, they are not often seen as most emerge from their holes or hiding-places only at night. Scuttling about in the dark, often with incredible speed, they follow almost directionless patterns in search of insects and other small animals. Raised off the ground, the long pedipalps are held forward as 'feelers' during this random search for food. Near their tips, sucker-like discs help to hold the prey or cling to steep rocky surfaces when clambering around stony areas.

Solifuges in the Park tend to be orange or orangey-brown, with bodies 20 to 50 millimetres long. The larger species, such as *Solpuga monteiroy,* are often fearsome in appearance with huge bodies and massive jaws. They have no poison glands, however, and tend to run away from rather than threaten any human. The huge jaws, found in all solifuges, are used to mash the prey to a pulp before sucking out the body liquids.

The long spindly legs so characteristic of these creatures are an ideal adaptation for their hunting existence, allowing them longer strides and greater speeds to overtake and capture their prey. If a solifuge blunders into view around your camp-fire, do not worry – it will streak off in fear as soon as you make your presence felt.

MILLIPEDES

Like unwieldy tanks barging ponderously ahead, these ungainly-looking animals with slow deliberate movements have a certain grace and beauty. They look like creatures Nature evolved as a cruel joke, but are, in fact, efficient and well-adapted for their way of life. Nature is no prankster, and they, too, have a contribution to make in her overall scheme. They help clear and transform dead and dying vegetation, slowly and inconspicuously chewing their way through the leaf-litter scattered on the bushveld floor, sometimes crawling to the upmost reaches of trees to reach the decomposing matter, rearranging the consumed elements and nutrients by delicate chemical processes within their bodies. Some of this food is used for their own well-being, the remainder passes through to feed the hungry hordes of bacteria ever-ready and waiting in the soil.

The Park has a rich variety of millipede species. Most of these are seen only in spring and summer, after a shower of rain or during cooler weather. Then they come out to feed by day, otherwise remaining in tightly curved balls below the soil or hidden in some tree-crevice or tiny cavern below a protective rock.

Most of the millipedes are dark, sometimes pleasingly banded with yellow or white. The outer surface of the body is covered with a tough protective armour to shield it from predators, the sun, and as a skeleton. To allow movement, the body has been divided into many segments, most of these each having two pairs of short legs. When walking, the legs move in a well-synchronized series of waves without which the creature would trip itself in a chaotic jumble of disorientated limbs.

Although the secretions of some species can cause severe pain if rubbed into the eyes, millipedes are completely innocuous and do not bite. If held in the hand they will normally curl into a tight ball and only unwind when placed back on the ground. Some species will try to frighten the captor with a totally harmless display of vigorous wriggling, the entire body contorted into a series of snake-like twists.

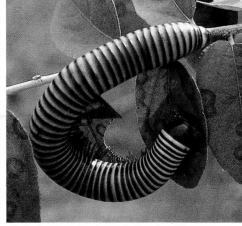

A solifuge builds its nest among fly puparia and hairs from impala carcass (left) and a millipede shows its protective rings of armour.

Its modified poison-injecting limbs are visible just behind the head of this centipede.

CENTIPEDES

In contrast with the millipedes, centipedes are nimble and rapid-moving carnivores which hunt down insects or similar small organisms. Not for them the rigid and inhibitive outer armour of millipedes; instead they have a softer, more leathery skin conducive to easier movement. They have reduced the number of legs to one pair per segment, lessening the chances of tripping themslves when running. The legs are also longer than those of millipedes, again an adaptation for greater speed.

Centipedes live under rocks or logs and in the shaded depths of leaf-litter well away from the drying rays of the sun, emerging at night to start their search for food. The first pair of legs just behind the head are hollow, and contain channels which allow venom from the poison glands to be injected rapidly and overcome the struggles of their prey. The poison is also used for defence, as when an unwary human places a hand on a centipede prowling on a piece of firewood. The effect of such a poison jab is a sharp pain much the same as a bee-sting.

Insects

In their sheer abundance and diversity, insects are the most successful of all living organisms, comprising more than 70 per cent of all earth's animal species. Even if all the different species of plants are added, insects still make up more than 50 per cent of all living organisms on our planet. They are so numerous and adaptable that they are man's only serious competitors for available food resources, each year consuming more than 10 per cent of our total output of agricultural products.

Fossilized specimens embedded deep in rocks prove that insects have existed for many millions of years, some, like the cockroaches, so well adapted that they have remained unchanged in general body shape and structure throughout this time. Others which could not adapt to the ever-changing environment slowly became extinct, but were replaced by insects which evolved better suited to new conditions.

With its warm climate and lush vegetation, the Park has a remarkable diversity of insect species spread in huge numbers over its entire area. These come in an amazing variety of shapes and sizes, some smaller than a pin-head, others almost as bulky as half a man's fist; others again thin but as much as 220 millimetres and more in length. Some (like many of the butterflies, moths, wasps, flies and dragonflies) are brightly and beautifully coloured, but most are so patterned and shaped that they blend inconspicuously into their environment.

All insects, however, play an important role in life's web. They may carry diseases which threaten human life – as is the case when mosquitoes transmit malaria and yellow fever; others also transmit diseases to other animals. Among these insects are the tsetse flies, horse flies, blow flies, sand flies, lice and fleas to list but a few. Vast quantities of crops or stored food products are destroyed each year by feeding insects, and millions of rands are spent on pesticides and other methods to combat them.

But these harmful species are by far the minority. The overwhelming majority of insects benefit man and the whole ecosystem. Their most important role is as pollinators, moving from one plant to the next, settling on a flower for a sip of energy-filled nectar, inadvertently gathering the pollen which will fertilize the stigma of the next flower on which they sit. So dependant on this process have many plants and insects become that the one cannot survive without the other. The most extreme examples of this are the fig trees, each of which species has a limited number of tiny wasp species able to fertilize it, because only these wasps are able to reach the plant's reproductive organs.

Dragonflies *(Odonata)*. Darting about the edges of rivers or pools, skimming low over the water, and at times poised quietly on the tip of some projecting vegetation, dragonflies are among the most attractive of all insects associated with watery environments. They are predators and use the large globular eyes which make up almost the entire head to locate and then track any prey which flies into view. Males are often territorial, aggressively chasing away other males.

Mating of these fairly primitive insects is elaborate and rather unusual. The male stores sperm in a pouch-like organ slightly behind the legs and on the underside of his body. He latches on to a female, holding her behind the head with a pair of claspers at the end of his abdomen, while she bends her abdomen forwards for its tip to come into contact with the sperm-pouch and fertilize her eggs – an acrobatic method of reproduction found only among the *Odonata*.

Hovering briefly just above the surface, the female dips her abdomen into the river or pool to lay her eggs. A few species, however, deposit their eggs on the stems of water-plants. After hatching, the larvae swim about seeking food, using unusual, long extensible cup-like jaws – which are shot out, much like a chameleon's tongue – to capture other small aquatic insects or crustaceans. Unlike most other aquatic insects, which use their legs to propel them, dragonfly larvae use the principle of jet propulsion. Water taken up into a pouch at the end of the body is squeezed out so forcefully that the insect is pushed rapidly forwards.

When full-grown the larva leaves its watery home and climbs a piece of waterside vegetation where a marvellous transformation takes place. Much as the worm-like caterpillar changes astoundingly to the radiant splendour of a winged butterfly, the squat larval body splits its upper side, and through this slit the adult emerges.

Cockroaches *(Blattodea)*. Everyone has his or her pet aversion, and many seem to have singled out cockroaches to occupy this unenviable niche. No doubt this stems from the nocturnal skitterings of those few species which scavenge crumbs and exposed food in many domestic dwellings. Yet these comprise only a minute fraction of the more than 3 500 species of cockroaches.

Usually found in and around rotting vegetation or on trees, they tend to be medium-sized insects, broad and flattened, with long antennae and a toughened triangular shield just behind the head. The legs are robust, often bristling with stout spines.

Although more closely related to termites, cockroaches like praying mantids produce eggs which are enclosed in an egg-case. This 'parcel' is either deposited in a protected crevice, cemented onto rocks or logs, or carried by the female wherever she goes.

Termites *(Isoptera)*. Generally regarded as primitive compared with most other insects, the termites' social habits make them fascinating. All the known species live in communities made up of various castes:

Left to right: Dragonfly *(Odonata)*; Cockroach *(Blattodea)*; and Termite soldier *(Isoptera)*.

usually soldiers, workers, and reproductives, though some termite species do not have workers, such duties in the colony being taken over by young reproductives, called pseudergates. These workers or pseudergates collect food, which is generally bits of plant material, feed the soldiers and reproductives, see to the well-being of the king and queen, and build, repair and maintain the nest. Their workload makes it essential that they greatly outnumber the other castes.

Soldiers have adapted to defend the colony, and rush out at the least sign of disturbance, often forfeiting their own lives to protect the others of the community. In most species the soldiers have large heads and very strong 'jaws' capable of inflicting a painful bite. However, in others the soldiers have a long 'snout' which sprays repellent or entangling fluids at any intruder which may threaten the community – a rather novel method of defence.

The reproductive caste is made up of winged termites which disperse to establish new colonies, usually in a mass emergence in spring or early summer, when hundreds, or even thousands, of individuals swarm out of the home colony to fly off clumsily into an unknown and perilous outside environment. Many are eaten – gulped down by frogs squatting at the exit holes, snatched in mid-air by birds which gorge on this unexpected feast, or dragged off by ants and other predators as they descend to the ground.

After landing, the males search frantically for females, who often emit a scent which aids the discovery. When, eventually, the female is found, the pair run off in tandem, female ahead, to find a suitable living place in the soil, under a rock or log, or in some similar protected position. Here they copulate and the female will lay some eggs which develop into worker and other termite castes, so that, in time, another colony is established. Of the many hundreds of reproductives which leave the original colony, only a very few successfully establish a new community.

Of the many species of termite in the Park, some live in underground tunnels, others in dry wood, but most noticeable are those which construct the huge characteristic pyramid-like mounds. Large mounds may contain a smoothly functioning community of more than a million termites. In the depths of the termitarium, as the mound is called, a vast network of galleries and chambers comprises the actual living quarters. One group has special chambers inside these mounds where termites cultivate a species of fungus on which they then feed. Most termites, however, consume dead plant material such as withered grass or decomposing logs. Most lack the enzymes which would enable them to digest properly the plant cellulose, and have instead evolved a mutually beneficial relationship, called mutualism, with very small single-celled organisms living inside their bodies. These micro-organisms digest the cellulose, retaining a small part of the resulting nutrients for their own sustenance while the remainder is utilized by the termite.

Stick Insects *(Phasmatodea)*. These show probably the best examples of camouflage in the animal kingdom. Long and thin, sometimes with knobbled or thorny outgrowths, these insects are shaped and coloured to resemble a twig or blade of grass. So astonishingly effective is their resemblance to their background that they are normally seen only when they move. Found in the trees or grass of the drier open bushveld, stick insects are more common than is often thought. Feeding on plant material, and very sluggish in their movements, they tend to live as solitary individuals. Using the large hind-wings tucked below narrow, hardened fore-wings, many species are able to fly, although their flight is clumsy and covers only short distances. The brightly coloured hind-wings are often suddenly flashed open to scare off threatening intruders.

Grasshoppers and Crickets *(Orthoptera)*. Although slightly different in appearance, grasshoppers and crickets share many characteristic features and habits, an indication that they are closely related in an evolutionary sense. The similarity of the enlarged hind legs adapted for jumping, the structure of the wings, mouthparts and many other organs, shows that somewhere in the past they had the same ancestors.

These insects abound in the Park, where the vast majority feed on plant material out on open land, though some have adapted themselves to life underground or have become predators on other insects.

Many species attract mating partners by sounds which are an important part of the courtship ceremony and which are made by rubbing serrated parts of their legs against ribbed portions of the abdomen or wings, or by rubbing their ridged wings over each other. This results in the surprisingly loud and sometimes incessant 'chirrrrrrrrr' so often heard in spring or summer. Grasshoppers have hearing organs situated slightly above and behind the last pair of legs, whereas crickets – equally strangely – have their 'ears' near the 'knees' of their forelegs.

Top: Stick insect *(Phasmatodea)* displaying remarkable camouflage colours and form.
Above left: Grasshopper *(Orthoptera)* laying eggs in soil. Right: Giant cricket *(Orthoptera)*.

As protection from predators, most species have become cryptically coloured, camouflaged in shape and colour to closely resemble their environment. Some katydid crickets have a remarkable resemblance to leaves, even the veins on their wings being structured to resemble those on leaves. A few species contain a bad-tasting substance which they advertise by bright and bold body colours in warning shades of red, black, and yellow. Predators soon learn to avoid these insects.

True Bugs *(Hemiptera)*. Although many laymen use the term 'bug' to describe all insects, it has a special meaning to zoologists and entomologists, referring to a specific group which includes cicadas, aphids, bed bugs and assassin bugs. All have long, tube-like mouthparts which are normally folded under the body, between the legs, when they are not feeding. Most sink these mouthparts deep into plants to suck the nutritious juices; others are predatory, jabbing their mouths into other insects or small animals and feeding on the body fluids.

The true bugs are very numerous and found in most environments. Several species live permanently in water, either skimming the surface on their highly elongate legs, or diving and swimming underneath the surface, like the water-boatmen whose short, flattened legs function as oars. Many of these aquatic bugs prey on insects which land accidentally in the water, or on mosquito larvae or other young which spend part of their lives submerged.

Aphids have fascinating and extraordinarily complex life cycles. Within a single species there may be sexual and non-sexual females, both capable of producing offspring. The sexual females copulate with males in the normal way so that genetic diversity is ensured by sperm fusing with the ova to be laid as eggs. By contrast, the non-sexual females do not copulate, but though unfertilized, produce live young by parthenogenesis – a process which also occurs in several other groups of insects. To further complicate matters, wingless aphids are produced at times, while at others winged aphids appear, these then flying off to ensure dispersal of the species. Many aphids are important transmitters of plant diseases, feeding on sick plants and infecting another plant when they settle down to suck its sap.

Ant Lions and Lacewings *(Neuroptera)*. Many adults of this group are superficially similar to dragonflies, having long bodies and two pairs of elongate wings criss-crossed with an elaborate network of veins. They are immediately distinguished by their easily visible antennae – unlike the dragonfly's which are short and very thin. At rest the wings are folded back over the body as a roof, whereas the dragonfly's project sideways, out from the body.

Most of the *Neuroptera* have strong mandibles with which to bite other insects on which they prey. The adults vary in form. Some have enlarged forelegs which lash out to grasp the prey; others have curiously long and clubbed antennae; while a few have very attractive, thin, tail-like hind-wings whose tips curl much like a corkscrew.

Long-horned ant lion *(Neuroptera)*, and (right) assassin bugs *(Hemiptera)* feeding on a millipede.

In appearance, the larvae differ totally from the adults. The ant lions found at the bottom of the conical pits dotted so liberally under many shady trees in summer are fairly representative of their shape at this stage of development. Ant lions construct their pits in soft soil by walking backwards in decreasing circles, flicking up their heads to throw out accumulated soil, until a pit shaped like an inverted pyramid is formed. Small insects stumble into these pits and are then caught by the ant lions waiting patiently submerged at the bottom. Not all larvae construct these pits; some roam above ground whilst others climb trees in search of prey. All have large jaws to catch and kill their prey.

Beetles *(Coleoptera)*. This, the largest single group of animals on earth, contains more than 330 000 different, already described species with many more still waiting to be discovered. In the Park numerous abundant species occur in and near rivers, in the open veld, on or under rocks, in logs and branches, in dung, in rotting carcasses, tunnelling below soil – some species even living as parasites in the bodies of other insects. Most species have a compact, robust body shape, the adults having hardened protective forewings under which the soft membranous hind-wings are folded.

Dung beetles are one of the more conspicuous and abundant groups seen in the Park, and the large elephant dung pads which so liberally litter many of the roads often attract great numbers of these insects. In spring and summer the freshly-dropped dung pads soon become a hive of activity, filled with beetles tunnelling and bulldozing their way inside. Some species use their forelegs and heads to form selected bits of the dung into a ball, rolling this away to be buried in the soil elsewhere. Some of the balls are eaten; inside others eggs are laid, one per ball. In these, the hatched larva feeds on the dung, leaving only a thin shell in which it pupates. Eventually the adult emerges from the

141

pupa, breaks out of the protective shell, and tunnels up through the soil to search for fresh dung and so restart the cycle. Other species simply tunnel into the soil beneath the dung pad, and construct chambers which are then stocked with dung. Eggs are laid in this and the adults then leave, blocking the entrance hole behind them.

By burying the dung these beetles benefit many plants and animals, for the soil is thus fertilized, allowing good plant growth which will then feed the herbivores. A less obvious, but equally important advantage, is that the dung does not remain in an intact mass on the surface where flies can lay their eggs, resulting in literally hundreds emerging after a week or two. Many of these spread disease, so that dung beetles contribute a great deal towards keeping the fly populations to an acceptable level.

Another fascinating group of beetles are the so-called 'fireflies' or 'glow-worms', occasionally seen near rivers or other water sources. Both sexes have luminescent light-emitting organs with which they attract each other. In many species the females are wingless and somewhat worm-like – hence the term 'glow-worms'. The light results when certain chemical substances are mixed in the body, and it is then reflected outwards by body crystals. The larvae are carnivorous, feeding mostly on snails and slugs, but the adults of most species do not eat, living only long enough to mate.

Flies *(Diptera)* Not only are flies the fourth largest group of insects in terms of their number of species, but they have a tremendous impact in the medical and veterinary fields. They transmit a surprisingly wide range of diseases and many species are parasites of man or other animals. Mosquitoes and tsetse flies – both of which suck blood – top the list of the disease-carrying flies in terms of their influence on man and animals. Every year malaria, transmitted by mosquitoes, still afflicts millions of people worldwide, whereas tsetse-transmitted nagana and sleeping-sickness still prevent man from exploiting exten-

Dung beetles *(Coleoptera)* rolling balls from droppings of impala (left) and blow fly *(Diptera)* feeding on flower of *Euphorbia*.

sive areas of Africa. Yellow fever, leishmaniasis, elephantiasis, encephalitis, and various enteric illnesses are only some of the other diseases transmitted by flies.

Because certain species transmit disease, mosquitoes have always attracted attention. Only members of the *Anopheles* group carry malaria, and are easily recognized as the adults rest with their heads close to a surface and the hind part of the body angled up and outwards. Females lay their eggs in pools of water, where the larvae feed on small bits of plant and animal offal. Like those of most other mosquitoes, the larvae and pupae drift just below the surface of the water, but are capable of vigorous wrigglings which propel them either away from danger or in search of food. Winged adults emerge from the pupae after a few days and, after drying their wings in the sun, fly off. Males feed on plant juices, but females need blood if their eggs are to mature.

When *Anopheles* suck blood from humans infected with malaria, the disease organisms, known as species of *Plasmodium,* invade first the intestinal lining and then the salivary glands of the mosquitoes where they complete an essential part of their development. If a human is bitten by such a mosquito, the malaria organisms are injected with the saliva into the blood of the host, and thence migrate to the liver. Here they multiply and after a while burst out of the cells to reinvade the bloodstream. It is at this stage, when the *Plasmodium* organisms are in the blood, that the typical symptoms of malaria develop (see also MALARIA, page 149).

There are also other blood-sucking flies which parasitize man and animals directly, like horse flies, bat flies and sand flies. Also important are the larvae, like those of the bot flies, which are internal parasites in the bodies of many animals.

But flies are also beneficial – more so than they are detrimental – acting either as pollinators of plants, as decomposers of animal and plant material (the larvae of many species feed on rotting substances, thus helping recycle nutrients), or as predators and parasites of other insect pests.

Flies have only one pair of wings, a modified second pair acting as flight stabilizers. These can be seen as small club-like organs projecting from the side of the body just behind the wings. The worm-like larvae live in a wide range of habitats – in fruit, inside leaves, in carcasses or dung, or as parasites inside the bodies of other insects or animals.

Most people view blow flies with revulsion, but, in fact, many species are of great benefit to us. Animals often die or are killed in dense vegetation where they lie undiscovered by vultures or hyenas. But the blow flies always find them, laying thousands upon thousands of eggs in the crevices and folds of the carcass. The resulting maggots quickly strip all the soft tissues and even dissolve large pieces of skin, in this way acting as highly effective scavengers, recycling the nutrients in the carcass and returning them to the ecosystem.

Top: *Charaxes* butterfly *(Lepidoptera)*. Centre left: Bagworm home *(Lepidoptera)*, and (right) diseased caterpillar *(Lepidoptera)*. Above left: Ants *(Hymenoptera)* feeding on the remains of a painted reed frog, and honey bee *(Hymenoptera)* gathering pollen (right).

Butterflies and Moths *(Lepidoptera)*.Of all the earth's multitude of insects, the magnificent beauty and showy splendour of butterflies and moths make them the most noticeable. But the brilliantly coloured species are in the minority; most are rather drab, in shades of brown, grey, or a mixture of other muted hues. Together, however, they form such an abundance of species that this is the second largest of the insect orders, only outnumbered by the beetles.

Butterflies and moths are characterized by their fairly large wings covered in very small overlapping scales. These scales, much like overlapping roof-tiles, are textured and sculpted to reflect the rays of the sun and so reveal the particular colours on the wings.

Another characteristic of most butterflies and moths is that their mouthparts have developed as a long, sucking tube which is coiled in a spiral below the head when not in use. Adults feed on nectar, or moisture from a wide range of other sources, such as dung, sap oozing from trees, or the muddy edges of rivers and pools.

Larvae of butterflies and moths have a typical caterpillar shape, and generally feed on leaves. Exceptions include the clothes-moths, for which cotton materials particularly provide a feast, and the larvae of certain moths which feed on the outer layers of animal horns.

Bagworms belong to the family Psychidae and derive their common name from the habits of their larvae. Using bits of vegetation, either twigs, grass, or pieces of leaves, they construct extraordinarily tough cases, or bags, padded with silk on the inside. The larvae live within these protective bags, dragging them along wherever they go, constructing new ones as they grow older and increase in size. Eventually they pupate inside these homes, and when the adults emerge the females find another use for the bags. Wingless, they emit a smell which drifts on the breeze to attract any males in the vicinity. These fly upwind to copulate with the female who is still partially concealed in her protective bag. Mating completed, she lays the eggs inside the bag, then dies later, having accomplished her most important life-task.

Numerous in the Park, butterflies gaily flit along river banks or out in the open bushveld. The swiftest are the multicoloured *Charaxes,* powerfully built with large muscles to drive the wings in flight. They are normally high-flyers which prefer the tree tops, settling to rest on a twig, or to feed on sap oozing from a small wound in the trunk. Often, however, they descend to earth to sip of moisture on an elephant dung pad, or drink quietly at the muddy edge of a river. A well-illustrated guide-book by Kloppers and Van Son (1978), on the butterflies of the Park is on sale in most of the rest-camps.

Wasps, Bees and Ants *(Hymenoptera)*. The *Hymenoptera* make up the third largest group of insects. Most of the adults have wasp-like shapes, the second segment of the abdomen constricted into a narrow-tubed petiole or stalk of variable length. The majority are important as crop and tree pollinators, and as parasites or predators on many insect pests. They even provide food in the form of honey.

145

Of the many species of wasp in the Park, some live in gregarious colonies sharing the tasks necessary to the smooth functioning of the community. They build combs, much like those of honey bees, laying eggs in the cells and stocking these with nectar and pollen to feed the young when they emerge. Most wasps, however, are solitary. They parasitize others' nests to lay their own eggs, make simple nests in twigs, against stones, in holes in the ground, or build highly attractive, pot-shaped mud cells. These nests are stocked with caterpillars, spiders, or other insects which the wasp has paralyzed with its sting, and the eggs are laid on this supply of food.

Bees are also abundant – not only the well-known honey bees, but a wide range of solitary and social species. Solitary bees, such as the carpenter bees which excavate their holes in wood, are similar in their habits to solitary wasps, except that the bees stock their nests with nectar and pollen as food. The nectar is used as a source of carbohydrates, whereas the pollen provides protein. Nectar is regurgitated by the adults as honey, so that actually the nests are stocked with honey and pollen. Many species of solitary bee make their nests in hollow twigs, using leaves or chewed-up plant material to separate the cells.

Of the social bees, mopane and honey bees are most commonly seen. Mopane bees, belonging to the genus *Trigona,* are abundant in the northern areas where they construct their nests in the hollow parts of mopane trees. The hive is entered through a short waxy tube, usually projecting from the trunk. Although these bees have no stings they can be bothersome in large numbers, for they settle on one's face and other exposed parts of the body, eagerly lapping up moisture, such as sweat, and sometimes blundering into the eyes.

Ants, varying in size and habit, are common throughout the Park. Many species are active by day, but several are nocturnal. The orange-brown sugar ants, *Camponotus,* for example, prefer to forage at night. Nests range widely in materials and situations; some built of pulped wood dangle from the branches of trees; some are tunnelled galleries in rotting wood; others are excavated holes in the ground; while yet others, like those of the army or driver ants, are temporary – the individuals simply cluster together.

All ants are social insects, with a colony structure that functions remarkably similarly to that of termites. Various castes (groups of individuals which are adapted to perform specific tasks) exist, so that again we find workers, soldiers, and reproductives. Similarly, there are mass emergences of winged reproductives which disperse in spring and summer.

Perhaps the most fascinating ants in the Park are the Matabele ants, found fairly commonly in the far north around Pafuri. Although not true army or driver ants, they march in long columns, up to seven abreast, in search of food. If the column is disturbed, these ants immediately break ranks to become a disorganized, aggressive mass of frantically-running individuals – all searching for the source of disturbance and capable of inflicting a very painful sting.

Accommodation

Demand for accommodation in the Park is always heavy, so it is advisable to make reservations well in advance. Bookings should be made through: 'The Chief Director, Reservations, National Parks Board, P.O. Box 787, Pretoria 0001'. As well as stating the number of adults and children in the proposed group, visitors should also indicate their preference of camps, the intended duration of their stay in each camp, and the type of accommodation they require. No deposit should accompany the initial application as this will be requested when accommodation has been reserved.

The reservations office will return a reservation voucher. This must be presented when entering the Park and at camps where you have booked accommodation. A small fee is levied on each car and all occupants above the age of six years, and this is paid at the entrance gate.

Reservations need not be adhered to strictly. The reception office in each camp will gladly enquire from other camps if suitable accommodation is available, and reservations may then be transferred to whichever camp you prefer.

Several different types of hut or housing unit are available in the various rest-camps scattered the length of the Park. Below is a guide to the types of accommodation offered, together with the code-letters used by the reservations office to denote these units. Clean bedding is supplied for all beds and camp staff clean the rooms daily.

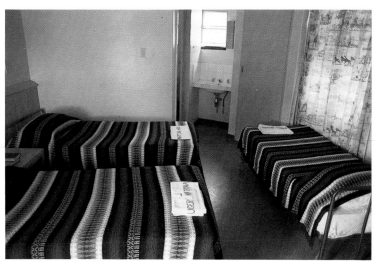

Interior of a standard G-type hut in Skukuza.

Although the following information is accurate at the time of this volume going to press, facilities and accommodation in the various camps may change.

Ordinary thatched huts (H). These vary in size and contain from two to six beds. In most camps, each unit has an air-conditioner, refrigerator and all have handbasins. They have no shower or toilet but all the huts are situated close to large ablution blocks. Ordinary huts are available at Pretoriuskop, Lower Sabie, Crocodile Bridge, Skukuza, Orpen, Balule, Olifants, Letaba and Shingwedzi.

Thatched hut with shower and toilet (G). This is the standard form of accommodation, is very pleasant, and consists of one room with two or three beds, air-conditioner (except at Shingwedzi and Punda Maria), refrigerator, shower, toilet and handbasin. Adjoining each is a verandah with table and chairs. They are available in all the camps except Crocodile Bridge, Orpen and Balule.

International Huts (NG). These are used to accommodate non-European visitors. Each comprises a pleasant room furnished with two to four beds and has a separate cubicle with shower and toilet. Most have a small kitchenette with gas stove, refrigerator, wash-up bay, but *no cutlery or cooking utensils*. These units are available at Lower Sabie, Skukuza, Satara, Letaba, Shingwedzi, Punda Maria and Berg-en-Dal.

Family cottage with kitchenette (F). These pleasantly arranged modern units each have two rooms with two or three beds. Each unit has an air-conditioner, shower or bath, toilet and handbasin. The small kitchen is supplied with a gas stove, refrigerator, wash-up bay, cooking and eating utensils. A verandah with table and chairs completes the unit. These are available at Pretoriuskop, Berg-en-Dal, Skukuza, Satara, Olifants and Punda Maria.

Family cottage without kitchenette (B). Similar to the above but without a kitchenette. They do have a small refrigerator, however, for keeping meat and drinks. Only available at Pretoriuskop.

Guest cottages. These are like typical holiday cottages found at seaside resorts. They are built with funds provided by private organizations or wealthy individuals who use these cottages for limited periods each year. For the remainder of the year they are hired to visitors as normal camp accommodation, but must be reserved three months in advance. All are fully supplied with kitchen utensils, bedding and the usual paraphernalia needed for comfortable living. Guest cottages are situated at Lower Sabie, Skukuza, Satara, Olifants, Letaba and Shingwedzi. Their sizes vary and they can accommodate from three to nine people.

The shop and reception complex at Skukuza.

Camping. Spacious camp-sites with large ablution blocks and kitchen units are available in all the camps. Visitors must provide their own tents or caravans.

Note: Nwanedzi, Roodewal and Malelane are small camps accommodating 15 people in cottages or huts. The camps must be reserved *en bloc* and supplies must be purchased in one of the other camps as there are no shops. All cooking and eating utensils are provided, however, as well as barbecue and washing facilities, bedding, and native staff to help around camp. For more details on these camps, see their full descriptions under 'CAMPS'.

Malaria. Malaria occurs sporadically during summer throughout the Park. It is caused by microscopic blood parasites transmitted by certain mosquitos and causes vomiting, general body ache and severe fever. Several people have died after contracting malaria in the Lowveld. Although the disease is fairly rare, it is nevertheless advisable to obtain preventative tablets, which are obtainable at most pharmacies. They are also on sale in the Park, but doctors recommend that a course of tablets be started prior to your arrival in the Lowveld. DO NOT BE OVERLY CONCERNED; if you take the anti-malarial tablets as prescribed you need have no fear of this somewhat over-rated illness. If you have not taken the tablets and develop the symptoms described, contact your nearest doctor and inform him you have been in a malarial area.

Restaurant interior, Letaba camp.

FACILITIES

Shops. All the larger camps, which excludes Malelane, Crocodile Bridge, Nwanedzi, Roodewal and Balule, have a well-stocked shop where meat, tinned and other food, beer and spirits, curios, medicines, film, cigarettes and a small range of books can be bought. Daily newspapers are available at Skukuza.

Restaurants. There are fully-licensed restaurants serving excellent food in all the larger camps. Dress for breakfast and lunch is informal, while elegantly casual clothes are worn for dinner. The service and atmosphere in these restaurants is very good.

Bank and Post Office. Skukuza is the only camp with a bank (Volkskas) and a Post Office. Volkskas will cash cheques drawn on most other banks provided the amount does not exceed R50,00. Travellers cheques and credit cards, such as Master and Visa cards, are accepted in all the shops, restaurants and reception offices for payments of more than R5,00.

Fuel and motor workshops. Oil and petrol are available at all restcamps except Nwanedzi, Malelane, Roodewal and Balule. Diesel fuel is obtainable only at Skukuza, Satara, Letaba, Shingwedzi, Lower Sabie, Punda Maria and Berg-en-Dal.

   The Automobile Association of South Africa provides vehicle breakdown services throughout the Park and has workshops for vehicle repairs at Skukuza, Satara, Letaba and Shingwedzi.

CAR RENTAL

Branches of Commercial Airways and Avis car rental established at Skukuza and Phalaborwa have placed the Kruger Park finally within reach of those previously hampered by distance and lack of time. The strategic location and effective combination of these commercial services make the Park more accessible than ever.

Avis is the only car rental company operating from within the Park and offers the usual range of vehicles, including mini-buses. Deliveries and collections of vehicles are made to and from any of the camps and areas immediately adjacent to the Park. There is no additional charge if a vehicle is returned to a different Avis branch. This arrangement is convenient as one can hire a car at Skukuza after flying in, spend time in the Park, and then either return the vehicle to Skukuza and fly to Johannesburg, or retain the car to drive to Johannesburg, viewing the scenery of the Blyde River Canyon and Lydenburg districts on the way.

Though there is usually no shortage of vehicles, it is advisable to reserve a vehicle at least three days in advance. Reservations can be made through any travel agent, Comair or Avis branch. To contact the Skukuza or Phalaborwa branches directly, the following numbers are applicable: Skukuza: telephone (0131252) 141; telex 2956 SA. Phalaborwa: telephone (01524) 5169; telex 42-3246 SA.

Avis staff meet all Comair flights, and private flights on request.

COMAIR FLIGHTS AND TOURS

An increasing number of people – particularly overseas business executives – fly to Skukuza for a few days of relaxation and game-viewing. With daily scheduled Comair (Commercial Airways) flights between Johannesburg's Jan Smuts Airport, Skukuza and Phalaborwa, visitors can fly in for a day's visit, or select from a range of flights to best suit their needs. Where parties are large enough special flights between Durban and Skukuza can be arranged.

Aircraft used by Comair are generally a 44-seater pressurised Twin Fokker Friendship or 11-seater Twin Cessna. Demand for seating on these flights is generally heavy so that advance reservation is advisable. These can by made by contacting: Comair Centre, Jan Smuts Airport, P.O. Box 7015, Bonaero Park 1622. For telephone reservations or general enquiries at the same centre the following numbers are applicable: telephone (011) 973-2911; telex 8-2375 SA or 8-4850 SA. Comair also has branches in Johannesburg, Welkom, Skukuza, Phalaborwa and Durban. Flight, hotel, tour and car hire reservations as well as bookings for other airlines can be made at any of these branches. Comair will also arrange passport or visa renewals, but these may take three days or more.

Comair also offers a range of 'Fly-in-Safaris' where visitors fly in to Skukuza or Phalaborwa, transfer to microbuses, and are conducted on tours hosted by couriers well-versed in the ways of the bushveld.

FLIGHTS AND TOURS FROM JOHANNESBURG

Tour CSK/1 *(one day)*. Fly to Phalaborwa and ten minutes after landing, enter the Kruger National Park in a microbus. Game-viewing drives with a stop at Letaba rest-camp for lunch. Return to Phalaborwa mid-afternoon for your return flight, arriving Jan Smuts Airport at dusk.

Tour CSK/1E *(one day, one night)*. 1ST DAY. Fly to Skukuza and transfer to a microbus to enjoy a full day's game-viewing. Overnight at Skukuza. 2ND DAY. After breakfast transfer to Skukuza Airport for departure to Johannesburg.

Tour CSK/2 *(two days, one night)*. 1ST DAY. Fly to Phalaborwa, transfer to luxury microbus and ten minutes later enter the Park. Game-viewing drives cover wide areas. Enjoy lunch, dinner and an overnight stay in one of the attractive guest lodges. 2ND DAY. Further game-viewing drives over an extensive area, returning to the airport in the afternoon for your return flight to Johannesburg.

Tour CSK/2E *(two days, two nights)*. Itinerary as for tour CSK/2 except that an extra night is spent in the Park and there is an additional early morning game-viewing drive. After breakfast transfer to Skukuza for flight to Johannesburg.

Tour CSK/2F *(one-and-a-half days, two nights)*. 1ST DAY. Fly to Phalaborwa. Transfer to microbus and view game en route to Letaba guest lodge. 2ND DAY. Game-viewing drives over a wide area and overnight stay in guest lodge. 3RD DAY. Early departure to Phalaborwa for flight to Johannesburg.

Tour CSK/2G *(two days, two nights)*. Itinerary as for CSK/2F except that on the third day additional game-viewing is enjoyed, returning to Phalaborwa for an afternoon flight to Johannesburg.

Tour CSK/3 *(three days, two nights)*. Itinerary as for tour CSK/2 except that an additional night and day is spent in the Park.

Tour CDK/3 *(two-and-a-half days, two nights)*. (Commencing Johannesburg, terminating Durban). Itinerary as for CSK/3 except that on Saturday, after the morning game-viewing drive, visitors depart from Skukuza on a flight arriving in Durban in the early afternoon. This tour is specially arranged for parties of about 20 visitors

Tour DCK/3 *(two days, two nights)* (Commencing Durban, terminating Johannesburg). 1ST DAY. Afternoon flight to Skukuza. Tea and refreshments at guest lodge. Late afternoon game-viewing and overnight in guest lodge. 2ND DAY. Full day game-viewing drives over a wide area. 3RD DAY. Depart from Skukuza on morning flight for Johannesburg. This tour is also by special arrangement only.

Twin Fokker Friendship with embarking passengers at Skukuza airport.

As well as the guided tours mentioned above, Comair also arranges safaris to private game parks bordering the Kruger Park. These include the well-known Mala Mala, Motswari, Londolozi, Sabi Sabi, Thornybush, Mananga, Umbabat, Inyati, Motswari M'Bali, Ngala, Harry's Huts and Tanda Tula game lodges. Although buses are normally used for these tours, return flight ferries can be arranged between Motswari, Ngala and Phalaborwa.

EDUCATIONAL

The Stevenson-Hamilton Memorial Library at Skukuza is well worth a visit. It has a large number of display cabinets filled with wildlife specimens, poaching equipment and a range of archaeological oddities as well as many books and magazines.

Open-air films on wildlife are often shown in the evening at many of the larger camps. The films have proved very popular and mostly deal with the general habits of animals found in the Park. Others are designed to inform visitors about research activities and projects.

In most of the rest-camp shops excellent guide-books on the large and small mammals, birds, fishes, reptiles, frogs and trees of the Kruger National Park are available.

At many of the camps there are information centres where visitors can view wildlife and other displays related to the Park.

In summer numerous rain-pools form, so that animals are more dispersed.

TRAVELLING HOURS

Like most other national parks, the Kruger Park has set times when visitors may travel outside rest-camps.

For their own safety, visitors must be in camp at night. Animals are easily blinded or startled by vehicles at night so that there is a considerable risk of serious accidents. The chances of people getting lost or stranded in remote areas is also increased at night. Poaching, always a problem, would also be encouraged by night-driving.

	Opening Time	Closing Time
January	5.00 a.m.	6.30 p.m.
February	5.30 a.m.	6.30 p.m.
March	5.30 a.m.	6.00 p.m.
April	6.00 a.m.	5.30 p.m.
May	6.30 a.m.	5.30 p.m.
June	6.30 a.m.	5.30 p.m.
July	6.30 a.m.	5.30 p.m.
August	6.30 a.m.	5.30 p.m.
September	6.00 a.m.	6.00 p.m.
October	5.30 a.m.	6.00 p.m.
November	4.30 a.m.	6.30 p.m.
December	4.30 a.m.	6.30 p.m.

Unless there is a good reason for being late, a fine may be levied for arriving after closing time.

The main entrance gates to the Park have the same opening and closing times as rest-camps except that in November, December and January they open at 5.30 a.m. All these main entrance gates are closed between 1.00 p.m. and 1.30 p.m.

GENERAL REGULATIONS

1. Because of the danger of disease transmission, *no pets of any kind may be brought into the Park.*
2. Poaching is a serious and ever-present problem in the Park, so all *fire-arms are to be declared at the entrance gate on arrival.* The tourist officer will seal the fire-arm and this seal will be removed when you leave the Park.
3. Wild animals are often unpredictable and frequently jump into the path of oncoming cars. It is therefore to your own benefit to *heed the general speed limit of 40 km/h.* Several traffic inspectors are present to ensure that traffic regulations are adhered to.
4. Outside a camp or picnic-site, for your own safety, *do not leave your vehicle or let your head, shoulders or arms protrude from the car window.* Animals sometimes appear tame, but many people have been injured by baboons or other animals scratching or biting exposed parts of the body. Lions have killed several tribesmen walking outside safe areas, so resist the temptation to walk about when not in camp.
5. Unfortunately, some people are still inclined to *remove or damage plants,* and *carving names and dates on trees* also persists. *Parks officials impose fines to discourage these habits.*
6. *Feeding of animals is misguided kindness.* Animals used to being fed often become aggressive and attack unsuspecting visitors who stop to admire but not feed them. Baboons and monkeys especially should not be fed.
7. *Discarding tins, paper and other refuse along the roads is unnecessary.* Besides being unsightly, this thrown-out garbage may also kill animals. Hyenas chew tins and damage their teeth or mouths, while other animals may swallow such refuse – leading to blocked or cut intestines. Rather carry a bag for rubbish inside the car.
8. *Keep to the designated tourist roads.* Should you venture onto a no-entry road and develop engine failure or other difficulties, it may be days before Parks officials locate you. Roads with no-entry signs don't lead to a magical paradise of animals; in most cases they are firebreaks which are seldom used and not suitable for passenger cars.
9. Most visitors come to the Park for peace, relaxation and to absorb the atmosphere of the wild. Be considerate of their needs and *don't play a musical instrument, radio or tape deck at a disturbing volume.*
10. Accidental fires cause great damage in the Kruger Park every year. *Be careful not to start* such *a fire* by throwing a burning match or cigarette-end out the window.

HINTS ON GAME-VIEWING

Everyone searching for game instinctively looks for a shape or colour which stands out from the background environment, or for movement which, if not caused by wind, can only be made by a living creature.

There are, however, certain useful hints to increase or improve the chances of finding game. The first and perhaps the most important point, is to decide what you want to see. There is no sense in spending days driving around the mopane scrub country of the Kruger Park if it is rhino you particularly seek. Consult the section on the distribution of mammals and then *concentrate on the areas you are likely to find the animals (birds or scenery) of your preference.*

Secondly, whether out to find particular animal species or for general game-viewing, *do not drive too fast.* Though the general speed limit in the Park is 40 km/h, that is the maximum permitted speed, *not* the best speed for game-viewing. Even from a slow-moving vehicle it is often difficult to notice a lion crouched low in the grass next to the road. In a car moving fairly fast, such opportunities pass totally unnoticed – and surprisingly often.

Early mornings, up to about 10.30 a.m., *and late afternoons,* from 3.00 p.m. onwards, *are the best time to find game,* as most of the medium- and larger-sized mammals are more active then. During the hot midday hours these animals stand quietly in the shade of trees, or lie down – making it difficult to see them. Early mornings and late afternoons are also more pleasant for driving, and the light is better for photography.

Most first-time visitors to the Park are eager to see lions. *The likelihood of seeing lions is greatly improved if you travel very early in the morning.* Lions are most abundant in the central area so try to make Satara one of your overnight stops if you are especially interested in seeing them. Try to be one of the first to leave when the camp gate opens in the morning, and follow any of the roads leading away from Satara. The chances of finding a pride of lion lying on the road at such a time are very good. Should you decide to wait until after breakfast the lions are almost certain to have been disturbed by earlier visitors and will have moved off into the bush.

For general game-viewing a good idea is to *wait at a waterhole and observe the animals as they come to drink.* Orpen dam and Mlondozi dam (near Tshokwane and Lower Sabie, respectively) have shaded lookout areas with chairs where visitors can relax and watch animals from the best vantage point. A wide variety of game can be seen under such conditions, and some lucky observers have also been rewarded in an almost grandstand situation by lions stalking and bringing down their prey.

Wilderness Trails

Many of us feel the occasional need to experience nature on a more personal and intimate level, and wilderness trails have been created to satisfy this. These trails afford one a closer look at the animals and plants we so often notice but never really see, to understand a little better how they live and grow together, and to experience the simple joy of being out in the open. Their rapidly growing popularity and the number of people who come back for more is a fair measure of the success of these trails.

There are three Wilderness Trails in the Park: the Wolhuter trail, which is roughly midway between Pretoriuskop and Malelane restcamps; the Olifants trail, along the Olifants river in the central part; and the Nyalaland trail in the north near the Luvuvhu river.

Each trail has its own base-camp where trailists stay overnight and from which daily walks are undertaken.

Trails are neither tests of endurance nor displays of strength or stamina. The ranger in charge adjusts his routine according to the composition of the party or their mood. Trailists undertake these trails for relaxation and enjoyment and the rangers do their best to provide just that.

Strolling in the immediate area of the Olifants Trail camp.

A maximum of ten, including the ranger and an assistant, usually take part, meeting on a Monday or Friday to set out by vehicle for the trails camp – three nights and two days in the wild.

All cooking and eating utensils are provided as well as beds and bedding. Simple, wholesome food is also provided.

Reservations for these trails can be made from: The Chief Director, Reservations, National Parks Board, P.O. Box 787, Pretoria 0001. It is best to provide some information on the number of people wishing to go, their ages, and a range of preferred dates for going on trail. Unfortunately these trails cannot cater for people aged under 12 or over 60.

THE WOLHUTER TRAIL

The base-camp for the Wolhuter trail lies between Malelane and Pretoriuskop amidst craggy hills separated by savannah-filled plains, waterholes and rivulets, far from the nearest tourist roads or other reminders of civilization. At the camp gate, tall tree fuchsias with outstretched branches welcome visitors and form part of the dense silver terminalia, sicklebush, bush-willow and marula vegetation into which the camp blends so well. It is not a camp which stands out abruptly as though rudely cut from the surrounding bush; instead it creates the impression that man-made structures have been sited with the approval of the natural bush. Paths wind their way around trees, not over their skeletal stumps; dwelling units and wash-up bays stand in the shadow of still dominant vegetation; here the bush has not been conquered, but man has entered by invitation.

The Wolhuter trail is best-known for the frequent sightings of broad-lipped (white) rhino – at close quarters. The rare mountain reedbuck are most numerous in this area, and impala, giraffe, wildebeest and lion are part of the scenery.

Bird-life abounds in this remote corner of the Park. Crested francolin boldly approach the camper drinking an early morning cup of coffee around the fire, to peck at the previous night's crumbs. Yellow- and red-billed hornbills land on the tables and chairs to join in the search for left-overs. In the trees around the fire-place barbets, doves, a variety of smaller birds and an occasional grey lourie chatter and cluck to imbue the camp with a tranquillity rarely found in today's world.

The Wolhuter trail is named after Harry Wolhuter, ranger for many years in the Pretoriuskop area, colleague and right-hand man to Colonel Stevenson-Hamilton during the formative years of the Park, and the man who, though severely wounded by a full-grown lion, managed to stab it to death with a hunting-knife.

THE OLIFANTS TRAIL

For scenic beauty and picturesque setting, the Olifants trail-camp is unsurpassed. The trail area covers a large slice of land immediately south of the Olifants river, near its confluence with the Letaba. Base-

Surging waters of the Olifants river burst through the narrow inlets which are overlooked by the Olifants Trail camp.

camp sits on an elevated natural embankment less than 300 metres from the swirling waters of the Olifants, and gives a magnificent view of the river and surrounding hills. Several majestic white syringa trees tower over the kitchen hut and tents, providing both shade and atmosphere, while the rustic reed-walled shower and toilet units lie tucked between a dense cluster of acacia shrubs. The toilet faces outwards from the camp's edge onto a rocky outcrop where klipspringer are occasionally seen.

Hornbills, bulbuls and barbets are common in and around camp, their chattering and melodious calls interrupting the incessant dull roar of the rushing river. Hippopotamuses lounge lazily on the sandy banks in full view of the camp, and numerous crocodiles bask in the sun or lie submerged in the river with only their eyes and nostrils visible. During the course of the day many animals arrive and depart after a refreshing drink of water. At night loud grunts and bellowing of hippo reverberate around camp to drown temporarily the soothing sounds of the crackling fire. During the pre-dawn hours the distant roar of lions never fails to evoke a contented sense that this, indeed, remains a piece of unspoilt Africa.

Walks may include a hike along the lily-laden waters of the Bangu river to any of the hills in the vicinity, or a ramble through fascinating surroundings to the junction of the Olifants and Letaba rivers.

Literally hours of enjoyment can by derived from clambering on and admiring the huge rocks below the camp. Here, aeons of surging waters have pitted, eroded, sculpted and smoothed the solid boulders into deformed works of art which provide endless pleasure and amazement. Scattered among these rocks are large pools of brooding water, while in the narrow passageways between them, streams of the broken river surge and seeth over waterfalls and through boiling maelstroms before reuniting to form again a single, gently flowing mass of placid water.

Trailists meet their ranger at Letaba camp at the start of the trails period and return to the same camp.

THE NYALALAND TRAIL

Sited on the banks of the Madzaringwe stream and shrouded by tall nyala and leadwood trees, the base-camp for the Nyalaland trail lies in a valley partly encircled by rocky hills studded with baobabs and other trees.

Appealing thatch-roofed wooden cabins stand in partial shade along the fence overlooking the stream. A thatched meeting area where trailists share their meals and sundowners stands beside a reed-walled kitchen unit. At the gate a gigantic baobab stands guard, its hollow interior offering refuge to a dozen or more mottled spinetail swifts, and the only recorded breeding site for this species in southern Africa.

Moving restlessly from tree to tree or warily hopping through the kitchen area in search of crumbs are hornbills, bulbuls, black fly-

Base-camp for Wolhuter Trail (left) and cabin and shower in Nyalaland Trail camp.

catchers and chinspot batis. Grey loeries watch inquisitively from the perimeter of the camp, loudly voicing their peculiar jeering calls. At night the drawn-out, haunting wails of hyenas occasionally interrupt the camp-fire conversation.

Because of the camp's location, trailists can walk in a range of vegetation types, each with its own faunal communities. Around camp, between the bouldered hills, the vegetation is a conglomeration of leadwood, baobab, tamboti, mopane, acacia, apple leaf, mahogany, bush-willow and several other species. The trail, meandering past the enchanting Tshalungwa spring where small fish dart about in pools fed by water seeping and bubbling from the earth below, lies in such mixed vegetation.

Further east, the scenery changes to mopane-dominated plains where zebra, kudu, impala, buffalo and elephant are often seen. A short distance to the north lies the Luvuvhu river where trailists walk under huge sycamore figs, Natal mahogany, jackal berry and nyala trees which share the banks with a large range of numerous other smaller trees unique to a riverine environment. Fish eagles often grace branches which reach out over the turbid waters, while rare black eagles soar silently between the high rock cliffs which in places rise steeply almost from the river's edge. In the shrubby undergrowth shy bushbuck and nyala daintily nibble at leaves, but rapidly bolt if trailists approach incautiously.

Trailists going to Nyalaland meet their ranger at Punda Maria and return to the same camp.

Camps

BALULE

Balule is a very small camp on the southern bank of the Olifants river near the causeway which crosses the river towards Olifants camp. Six rustic huts, five of which are available to visitors, each hold three beds, but showers, handbasins and toilets are all located in a shared ablution block. Ten sites are allocated for tents and caravans. Firewood, barbecue facilities and a freezer are also provided.

Situated off the main road, Balule has a privacy and character divorced from the busy hustle and bustle of the larger camps. The sounds of hyena, hippo and lion often pierce the nocturnal quiet and, when heard from the spartan atmosphere of this camp, take on a more personal meaning than they do among the civilized, modern conditions so prevalent in most other camps.

There is no shop, fuel station or reception office at Balule, so that all food and other requirements must be obtained from either Letaba, Olifants or Satara.

When reservations have been made for Balule, check in at the Olifants camp reception office before taking up your accommodation.

Balule lies in a transitional zone between the knobthorn-, marula- and leadwood-dominated central plains and the mopane-covered flats of the northern half, so it is wise to consult the descriptions of vegetation and animals listed under camps like Satara and Letaba before deciding in which direction to travel in search of game.

BERG-EN-DAL

Berg-en-Dal is the first of a series of new camps planned to relieve the ever-increasing demand for accommodation in the Park. In Afrikaans it means 'Mountain-and-Dale', an appropriate name for this medium-sized camp situated in the wooded hills between Malelane and Pretoriuskop.

The camp will be spread on the banks of the Matjulu stream, roughly 12 kilometres west of Malelane, and should be completed early in 1984. With its many facilities and view across the stream and nearby dams where animals congregate to drink, Berg-en-Dal should prove to be one of the most popular camps.

It will comprise 69 G2- and G3-type huts offering luxury accommodation, and scattered between the many trees will be a further 23 self-contained family cottages, each with two three-bedded rooms. Unique to this camp, the tent and caravan areas will be separate, with 40 sites for caravanners, and 20 sites allocated for tents. Modern kitchen units and ablution blocks will be conveniently situated.

Balule camp (left) and Olifants river in flood.

Housed in separate buildings but forming part of the same large complex, will be a shop, restaurant, snack-bar, lounge, conference hall, and information centre. The reception office stands apart in another part of the camp.

Diesel will be sold at the fuel station.

An added attraction for many will be the swimming pool.

CROCODILE BRIDGE

Crocodile Bridge is an old, fairly small camp with a rustic, quiet character which holds particular appeal for honeymoon couples and the elderly. Like Malelane, it serves as an entrance gate, and lies near the edge of the Crocodile river.

There is no restaurant at Crocodile Bridge so overnight visitors should bring their own food, which can be prepared in the kitchen located near the centre of the camp. A small range of tinned foods and other essentials are on sale in the reception office. Tea, coffee, sandwiches or other refreshments are not available, but cool drinks are sold at the fuel station.

There are twelve three-bedded huts and eight two-bedded huts as well as 12 sites for campers. The tarred road from Lower Sabie goes through the camp to link with the national highway at Komatipoort, 13 kilometres south of the river.

Driving from the camp towards Lower Sabie one enters essentially flat and fairly open country dotted with mainly knobthorn acacia and marula trees. Wildebeest, zebra, impala, giraffe, warthog and kudu are all common, and the chances of seeing buffalo, lion and cheetah are also good. Roughly eight kilometres from camp along the road to Malelane is a pool which a herd of hippos has made its home and spends much of the day lazing on a sand-bank in open view. Elephant and other animals often come to drink here so, with a little luck, these may also be seen. A Bushman painting from some bygone age adorns the rock cliff which overlooks the hippo-pool.

163

Letaba.

LETABA

Another of the larger camps, Letaba is spread along the southern bank of the river from which it takes its name. Many regard this as their favourite camp because of its quality of relaxed restfulness.

Tall mlala palms – from which local tribesmen derive an intoxicating liquor by allowing the extracted juices of the tree to ferment – add a tropical touch and share the camp grounds with gnarled apple leaf trees, Natal mahogany and thorny acacias. Short-cropped lawns cover the area between huts, and aloes grace the several rock gardens placed around camp.

Gazing across the fence to the river below, the visitor can observe an endless rhythm of animals arriving to drink and then moving on. Elephant spend a great deal of time browsing and lounging in the river-bed in full view of camp.

Accommodation offered at Letaba consists of the following:

Type of hut	No. of huts	No. of beds/hut	Shower/bath & toilet
G3 (with gauze-enclosed verandah)	22	3	Yes
G3 (with open verandah)	25	3	Yes
G3 (with ramp for paraplegics)	1	3	Yes
H3	25	3	No
H4	12	4	No

As well as these there are six international huts (code: NG3) each with three beds, shower and toilet, and kitchenette, but no cutlery or crockery is supplied.

A two-roomed unit is available for maids or chauffeurs.

The Melville guest cottage is completely self-contained and can house a maximum of nine people, and a camping area with its own ablution block and kitchen unit has space for 20 caravans or tents. A coin-operated laundromat with tumble-drier is also available.

The reception office adjoins the shop where food, liquor, cigarettes, curios, films and household medicines are sold.

Letaba has one of the most beautiful restaurants in the Park. The large building contains a dining area, bar counter, lounge where refreshments are served, and a long verandah which provides a beautiful view of the river.

Near the fuel station, where diesel is also available, the Automobile Association (A.A.) has a small workshop with breakdown facilities.

Letaba is ideally situated for those who wish to see the contrasting northern and southern areas. North from the Letaba river vast stretches of mopane-covered plains roll onwards past Shingwedzi to Punda Maria. Elephant, zebra, tsessebe and waterbuck are often seen, while ostriches and the rare roan antelope occasionally make an appearance.

To the south, beyond the Olifants river, lie the marula- and acacia-dominated plains of the central area. Herds of zebra and wildebeest roam the veld with kudu, giraffe, impala, buffalo and elephant. Lion and cheetah are also frequently seen.

The gravel road which meanders along the river and leads to Olifants camp provides a pleasant short drive offering splendid scenery and a better-than-average opportunity of seeing lion and klipspringer.

LOWER SABIE

A lovely setting, ideal size and great natural beauty, make this camp extremely popular with visitors at any time of the year. The camp lies on a slight elevation along the banks of the Sabie river, affording an excellent view of its waters. In the evening animals can be seen coming to drink, while buffalo and elephant often feed on the reed-fringed banks of the river.

The camp is neither too big nor too small – comparable in size with Olifants, Letaba and Shingwedzi – to satisfy the needs of most people. Green, well-tended lawns grace the areas between huts and tall shady broad-leaved trees help make the camp an oasis for relaxation and enjoyment.

Accommodation in the camp is made up as follows:

Type of hut	No. of huts	No. of beds/hut	Shower/bath & toilet
G2	58	2	Yes
H1	4	1	No
H2	14	2	No
H3	12	3	No
H5	6	5	No
NG3	2	3	Yes

Lower Sabie (top left), Malelane (left) and impala rams, horns locked in battle (right).

Large ablution blocks are strategically located to serve huts without showers and toilets. All huts have handbasins, air-conditioners and refrigerators. Four bungalows, each with four beds, are available for chauffeurs and other servants.

There are three fully self-contained guest cottages in camp. The Rive and Moffatt cottages each accommodate four people and the Keartland cottage can take seven.

The camping area has 27 stands for tents or caravans, two of these being reserved for use by non-Europeans. Large kitchens with gas stoves and wash-up facilities are also available.

Lower Sabie, without doubt, is located in one of the prime areas for game-viewing. The greater part of the surrounding area is made up of flat plains covered with acacia, marula, leadwood, bush-willow and several other species of trees, with a thick grass cover between. The vegetation is not too dense, so that finding and viewing animals is fairly easy. Because of the many waterholes, abundant grass and foliage, a large number of animals comprising many species are found in the area. Not far from camp in a northerly direction lies the Mlondozi dam. Ducks, herons and kingfishers are always present and many animal species continually visit the dam, where hippo and crocodile can also be seen. South towards Crocodile Bridge lies the Mhlanganzwane dam, another favoured drinking site for animals in the vicinity. To the west lies the tarred road leading to Skukuza, closely twisting its way along the Sabie river and known to be very good for finding bushbuck, leopard and lion.

MALELANE

Close to the new Malelane gate, this small private camp has been retained as a relic of the original Malelane rest-camp of earlier years. It accommodates a maximum of 19 people, and must be reserved as a whole. Five luxury huts, four with four beds and one with three, form a neat crescent in spacious, well-kept grounds.

There is no shop, restaurant or snack-bar, but a large outside kitchen has a stove, refrigerator, freezer and wash-up facilities. Fuel and other supplies must be obtained from other camps in the vicinity, such as Berg-en-Dal.

From Malelane a tarred road leads to Skukuza and links with good gravel roads to Pretoriuskop and Crocodile Bridge. All these roads wend their way through country which is stocked abundantly with animals such as impala, kudu, giraffe and warthogs, while zebra, wildebeest, rhino, buffalo, lion, cheetah and wild-dogs are also frequently seen.

NWANEDZI

Situated near the border with Moçambique, Nwanedzi lies on the banks of the lily-clad river after which the camp was named. In Shangaan this name refers to 'reflections of the moon'. Not far beyond the river, craggy euphorbia-covered peaks of the Lebombo range rear up to add some of the character and peace only mountains provide.

The camp itself is small, providing accommodation for a maximum of 15 people. There are two bungalows, each with two beds, built-in cupboards, a shower, toilet and handbasin. At the upper end of the camp is a large cottage with toilets, shower, bathroom and 11 beds. There is an enclosed outside kitchen, with a refrigerator, and a little summer-house for lounging completes the camp's facilities.

Nwanedzi camp is a short distance off the main road which leads to the Nwanedzi lookout point, so that the camp is secluded and totally private. Two camp attendants keep the camp tidy, and though preparing food or washing clothes are not part of their official duties, they will do so for a small gratuity.

The camp must be reserved and occupied by one party, which can be made up of any number to 15 maximum. A group of ten or fewer is charged a basic fee, with an additional charge for each extra person.

All bedding and kitchen utensils are provided, but there is no shop so visitors should bring their own food. The nearest fuel station and shop are at Satara, under whose management Nwanedzi falls and where visitors should first check in.

Wildebeest, zebra, kudu, giraffe, impala and warthogs are all common on any of the drives in the area around Nwanedzi, and ostriches are known to be fairly plentiful. The gravel road (S41 and S100) leading back to Satara along the river is particularly rewarding as buffalo, elephant, lion and leopard are frequently seen.

Part of the magnificent view from Olifants camp.

OLIFANTS

Sprawled across the uppermost levels of a steep cliff which rises from the northern bank of the Olifants river, this beautiful camp commands an unequalled panorama. Aloe-dotted stony terraces separate the huts spread over the hill-top site. Many huts lie snuggled near the very edge of the cliff, giving a magnificent unobstructed view, while enough tall mopane and other trees ensure that at least some of the atmosphere of the bush still reigns in the camp.

From the lookout point just below the restaurant/shop complex, many animal species may be seen coming to drink, and at night the distant sounds of hippo are a constant reminder of the river below.

In the centre of camp a large building houses the reception office, self-service restaurant, a verandah where tea, coffee and snacks are served, rest-rooms, and a shop selling the usual range of curios, food, liquor, film, cigarettes, and some commonly used medicines.

Olifants is one of the larger camps and has the following accommodation for visitors:

Type of hut	No. of huts	No. of beds/hut	Shower/bath & toilet
G2	36	2	Yes
G3	27	3	Yes
Family cottage	2	4	Yes
H2	15	2	No
H3	15	3	No
H4	6	4	No

There is also a six-bedded family cottage with its own fully equipped kitchenette, and two G2-type huts are available for paraplegics. Maids and chauffeurs can be accommodated in two rooms, each with four beds, and the Ellis guest cottage, with four bedrooms all with bathroom *en suite,* is available to visitors for most of the year.

The camping area with its own ablution block, kitchen unit and barbecue facilities has 15 sites for tents and caravans.

A so-called 'special camp' to one side within the main camp has six huts, each with three beds, a shower, bath and toilet. Adjoining these is a conference hall which can comfortably seat at least 50 people.

Near the fuel station, wildlife exhibits and photographs are displayed in a small museum-cum-information centre. Alongside it is an amphitheatre where wildlife films are frequently screened in the evenings.

Visitors staying over at Olifants are ideally based for game-viewing drives. To the south of the river lie the rolling plains of the central area where herds of zebra and wildebeest grace the horizon, and giraffe, impala, kudu, buffalo, and elephant are common. Lions and cheetah are sometimes seen on the drive to Satara.

To the north of Olifants the vegetation changes rapidly until a solid mass of mopane trees covers the landscape. Zebra, impala, kudu and elephant are common, and klipspringer are sometimes seen on the rocky hills which occasionally break through the sea of mopane vegetation.

The river drive, which initially follows the Olifants and then the Letaba rivers, is rewarding in its scenery and animals.

ORPEN

Named in honour of the Orpen family, who in the earlier part of this century donated large tracts of land and sums of money to the infant Kruger Park for the construction of much needed waterholes, this small camp with an entrance/exit gate straddles the boundary directly due west of Satara.

Standing in the dry open plains of the central area, it is permeated with the unhurried restfulness so characteristic of the bushveld. In camp, tall acacias and marula trees share the grounds with red bushwillows, while small rock gardens overgrown with aloes and Barberton daisies separate the huts.

Orpen Camp (top) and Pretoriuskop.

A small shop, which also serves as a reception office, sells curios, food, cigarettes, liquor, film and wildlife books. There is no restaurant in this camp, but a kitchen unit where visitors can prepare their own food is available. Fuel can be obtained near the gate.

Orpen camp has ten huts, each with two beds (code: H2), and two huts with three beds in each (code: H3). None of the huts have showers or toilets, but an ablution block is conveniently situated nearby.

There is no camping area inside Orpen, but the nearby Marula 20-caravan camp, which overlooks the Timbavati river, falls under the management of Orpen, where caravanners should first check in.

The surrounding area offers excellent opportunities for game-viewing. On the drive to Satara herds of zebra and wildebeest graze next to the road, while giraffe, impala, warthog and elephant are common. Turning off from this road to follow the Timbavati river northwards through pleasant scenery to Olifants camp, lion, cheetah and leopard are likely to be seen.

Driving south in the direction of Mzanzene and Hlangulene picnic-sites, magnificent sable antelope are often seen.

170

PRETORIUSKOP

The third largest camp in the Park, Pretoriuskop lies nestled in the south-west corner in hilly country where several rocky outcrops and ridges break the horizon around camp. Like all the other camps, with the possible exception of Skukuza, Pretoriuskop is calm and restful. It is spacious with large lawn-covered areas partially shaded by tall marula trees, Natal mahogany and several other species. A swimming pool made from natural rock abuts the south side of camp. Here children and adults can splash after a hot and dusty drive in summer.

The following accommodation is available to visitors:

Type of hut	No. of huts	No. of beds/hut	Shower/bath & toilet
G2	15	2	Yes
G3	31	3	Yes
G4	3	4	Yes
Family cottage (self-contained)	5	6	Yes
Family cottage (no kitchenette)	2	6	Yes
H1	12	1	No
H2	34	2	No
H3	16	3	No
H5	5	5	No
H6	1	6	No

An additional 30 H2-type huts are available for block-booked school tours.

The camp also has a 'caravan home' with five beds, bath, toilet and kitchenette supplied with cutlery and crockery.

There is no international accommodation, but two H4-type huts are available for maids or drivers accompanying visitors.

The camping area has 50 sites for tents and caravans.

A small but spacious restaurant has a warm, intimate atmosphere, and the nearby shop is well-stocked with food, curios, liquor, tobacco, books relating to the bushveld, and the more common household medicines. There is a coin-operated public telephone near the reception office.

Pretoriuskop lies in an area with a relatively high annual rainfall, so that a distinct vegetation zone has developed. The dominant trees are silver terminalia, sicklebush and marula, with a dense undergrowth of tall thatching-grass often up to two metres high.

Several roads criss-cross the area around camp, twisting their way between hills and through tall grassveld, providing a choice of short early morning or late afternoon drives. As well as the normal widespread mammal species, the possibility of seeing rhino and sable antelope is good.

Many visitors make Pretoriuskop their last night-stop before leaving through Numbi Gate.

PUNDA MARIA

Punda Maria is one of the gems among the camps. Removed from civilization, here one can 'feel' the wildness of the remote bushveld.

The camp lies in tiers on the slopes of a large hill and looks down on mopane-filled plains pimpled with several other hills. The attractive, long huts which make up this fairly small camp stand on terraces while the spacious camping area is spread along the base of the hill.

The following accommodation is offered:

Type of hut	No. of huts	No. of beds/hut	Shower/bath & toilet
G2	18	2	Yes
G3	4	3	Yes
Family cottages	2	4	Yes

The G3-type huts and family cottages each have a kitchenette provided with cutlery and crockery, and the camping area, with 25 stands for tents and caravans, has two kitchen units and two ablution blocks.

A new double-storeyed complex contains the reception office, restaurant, Nyalaland trails office, rest-room, a small information/display room, and a shop selling the usual items.

From Punda Maria the best drive for game-viewing is through the mopane flats to the Luvuvhu river at Pafuri. Along the way impala, zebra, buffalo and elephant can be seen, while eland and sable antelope also make an occasional rare appearance. Nyala are common on the river roads in the Pafuri area, and shy bushbuck inhabit the dense undergrowth below towering sycamore fig, Natal mahogany, jackal berry and nyala trees on the banks of the Luvuvhu. Numerous crocodiles laze on the many sand-banks, and abundant vervet monkeys and baboons provide an endless source of amusement.

In the evening, just before closing time, it is worthwhile taking a short drive along the Mahonie loop road to a small waterhole behind the hill on which Punda Maria sits. Bateleur eagles sometimes perch on the dead tree next to the pool, while saddlebill storks, hadedah ibises and Egyptian geese often stroll in the shallow water.

A few kilometres south of the camp visitors can leave the Park through Punda Maria Gate, following the road which passes through the Republic of Venda to Louis Trichardt. No passport is required.

ROODEWAL

Situated on the bank of the Timbavati river, this attractive private camp lies roughly halfway between Satara and Olifants. Very small, it accommodates a maximum of 15 people and must be reserved *en bloc*. It is managed in the same way as Nwanedzi, but falls under the control of Olifants camp. The grounds contain a fully-equipped family cottage with six beds, and three G3-type luxury huts with three beds,

Punda Maria has a charming setting.

and a shower and toilet. An outside kitchen unit with refrigerator and stove is conveniently situated.

There is no shop or fuel station in camp, but Olifants, Satara and Orpen are all within easy travelling distance for supplies.

Roodewal is in the transitional zone between the knobthorn/marula-dominated grassy plains of the east, and the more densely wooded, mixed bushwillow/mopane veld of the west. Its location provides tremendous scenic drives and sightings of a wide range of animal species such as kudu, zebra, wildebeest, impala and elephant, while lion and leopard are also often seen.

SATARA

Second in size only to Skukuza, Satara lies near the centre of the vast plains between the Sabie and Olifants rivers. The camp is surrounded by flat, grass-filled country dominated by tall knobthorn, acacia and marula trees. Despite its size, the camp retains a tranquil atmosphere with none of the impersonal detachment so often associated with a large camp. Tall marulas and acacias punctuate its grounds and broad-leaved Natal mahogany and sausage trees cast their cooling shadows over the lawns and huts.

Bird-life is profuse and large numbers of starlings, buffalo weavers and house sparrows fly about between the huts in search of crumbs. Hornbills peer from their tree-top perches, occasionally venting their mocking staccato calls. In winter black-headed orioles and sunbirds provide a spectacular sight as they feed at the flowers of the numerous aloes growing here.

A small waterhole has been created just off the restaurant side of the camp, so that visitors can observe animals as they come to drink.

Accommodation available at Satara consists of the following:

Type of hut	No. of huts	No. of beds/hut	Shower/bath & toilet
G2	94	2	Yes
G3	50	3	Yes
NG3	4	3	Yes
Family cottage	10	6	Yes

Four of the G2-type huts have been adapted for the use of paraplegics. Family cottages all have their own kitchenette equipped with cutlery and crockery. The NG3-type huts have a toilet, shower, air-conditioner, kitchenette and refrigerator, but no cutlery or crockery. Two four-bedded huts provide accommodation for maids or chauffeurs.

The camping area has a minimum of 30 sites, all conveniently situated near ablution blocks, kitchens and barbecue facilities. There is also a coin-operated laundromat.

A large self-service restaurant providing excellent food is situated in the graceful building which also houses a self-help snack-bar, restrooms, the reception office, and a shop stocked with curios, tinned and refrigerated foods, books, liquor, cigarettes and films.

The Automobile Association (A.A.) has breakdown facilities and a small workshop at Satara. Diesel is also obtainable at the fuel station.

The plains of the central district surrounding Satara are filled with large herds of zebra and wildebeest, and kudu, giraffe, impala, waterbuck and many other species of mammal are abundant. Elephant and buffalo are common, and this region boasts a higher population of lion than any other part of the Park. Leopard are frequently seen along the road following the Nwanedzi river, which flows past Satara just south of the camp.

SHINGWEDZI

Tucked between tall mopane trees and facing onto the Shingwedzi river, the camp lies in the scrub-filled plains of the far north. It is medium-sized and has large spacious grounds which seem to capture some of the atmosphere of remoteness so different from that of its southern counterparts. Small rock gardens with aloes and impala lilies stand beside fan-shaped mlala palms which grow clumped all around the camp.

A large complex – housing the reception office, restaurant, restrooms, self-help cafeteria, a shop which sells food, liquor, cigarettes, curios, film and household medicines, and a small information/display centre – overlooks the tree-lined river below.

Shingwedzi has the following accommodation:

174

Type of hut	No. of huts	No. of beds/hut	Shower/bath & toilet
G2	12	2	Yes
G3	34	3	Yes
G3 (for paraplegics)	2	3	Yes
H2	12	2	No
H3	12	3	No

There is also a self-contained guest cottage which can accommodate eight persons.

An international family cottage will sleep four, and two international G2-type huts each have a fully equipped kitchenette.

Eight stands for non-Europeans and 26 for Europeans are available for tents and caravans. Kitchen units and ablution blocks are conveniently situated close to these camping areas.

The Automobile Association (A.A.) has a small workshop at Shingwedzi with breakdown facilities, and diesel is sold at the fuel station.

Game-viewing drives from Shingwedzi mostly pass through flat mopane country where impala, zebra, elephant, buffalo and sometimes sable, roan antelope and tsessebe are seen. Waterbuck are often found around the waterholes.

Towards Punda Maria a gravel road which turns off from the tarred road closely follows the Mphongolo river. Along this drive impala, elephant, kudu and waterbuck are often seen, and nyala frequently provide a pleasant surprise.

The best game-viewing drive from Shingwedzi, however, is the gravel road which follows the Shingwedzi river in a south-easterly direction towards Letaba. Along this road animals, especially waterbuck, are abundant. The Kanniedood dam, which lies beside the same road, always provides worthwhile viewing, with darters abundant here as nowhere else in the Park, sitting on the many logs which jut from the water, spreading their wings to sun themselves. Kingfishers, herons, storks and ducks are also common.

SKUKUZA

Meaning 'complete changeabout' or 'he who sweeps clean', Skukuza was the name which his African staff gave Colonel James Stevenson-Hamilton, the first warden of the Sabie Game Reserve and eventually the Kruger National Park. By far the largest camp, it is also the operational and administrative headquarters of the Park.

Inevitably, because of its size, Skukuza has lost much of the intimacy that allows the visitor to identify and feel part of the surrounding wilderness. Only the placid waters of the gently flowing river in front of the camp instil an atmosphere of relaxed peacefulness. Nevertheless, Skukuza is a very popular camp because of its accessibility by road and air, and its favourable location for viewing a number of animal species.

Skukuza camp is fronted by a gently flowing Sabie river.

Skukuza offers the following accommodation:

Type of hut	No. of huts	No. of beds/hut	Shower/bath & toilet
G2	74	2	Yes
G2 (for paraplegics)	2	2	Bath and Toilet
G3	68	3	Yes
Family cottage	1	4	Yes
Family cottage	4	6	Yes
H2	20	2	Yes
H3	18	3	No
H4	12	4	No

The family cottages mentioned are all self-contained and provided with cutlery and crockery.

A small international camp has four huts, each with four beds, a shower and toilet; and three huts each with four beds, a shower, toilet, kitchenette, but without cutlery or crockery. In the same area space is provided for 10 caravans or tents.

There are three self-contained guest cottages in Skukuza camp. The Struben Cottage has accommodation for six, the Monis Cottage for nine, and the Lion Cottage for only two people.

A large camping area with kitchen units, ablution blocks and barbecue facilities has 50 sites for tents and caravans.

To accommodate school tours, a building divided into dormitories can comfortably fit 64 children. Teachers or supervisors have two huts nearby, each provided with two beds. This complex also has its own dining-room where meals prepared by the Park staff are provided.

A conference room, which can seat approximately 30 people, has an adjoining kitchen with grills, stoves and refrigerators, although meals from the main restaurant can also be served to delegates.

Near the fuel station, where diesel fuel is available, the Automobile Association (A.A.) has a well-equipped workshop capable of undertaking most vehicle repairs. Breakdown facilities are also available.

Volkskas Bank has a small agency near the reception office and will cash cheques drawn on most other banks for amounts not exceeding R50,00. Comair has an office at the airport a few kilometres away. Daily flights arrive and depart to and from Jan Smuts Airport.

A large modern post office with several public telephones is part of the complex which houses the reception office and a shop selling curios, food, liquor, cigarettes, film, household medicines, books and daily newspapers. Adjoining the shop is a spacious restaurant, complemented by a snack-bar which leads off the verandah where drinks are served in the evenings. The new Train Restaurant is a novel idea which should appeal to many. It consists of a converted dining and lounge car situated on a portion of the historic Selati railway line. A la carte meals are served, and 44 people can be accommodated at each sitting. Drinks are served in the adjoining lounge. In front of the impressive Stevenson-Hamilton Library – which is always worth a visit – is an amphitheatre where wildlife films are screened.

Skukuza is situated in bushveld dominated by red bush-willow and acacia. Drives along any of the surrounding roads are certain to produce sightings of a wide range of animals and birds. Impala, kudu, giraffe, steenbok are common, while lion, elephant, wild-dogs and leopard are all regularly seen.

Perhaps the best drive is that along the river to Lower Sabie camp. Luxuriant vegetation covers the river banks and provides a home for animals such as bushbuck, leopard and even a few nyala. Hippo and crocodiles adorn the sand-banks and rocky shores adjoining the river, and can be seen from the gravel roads which twist off the tarred road to wind beside the river for a short distance. Bird-life is abundant.

Recommended routes

This section is intended particularly for overseas visitors and others who often have only a few days to spend in the Kruger Park, yet wish to see as much as possible.

The recommended routes are intended to provide the best opportunity of seeing the most mammals and birds of as many species as possible, the best scenery, and suggest the most convenient accommodation. They are also designed to cover as much of the Park as possible – thus the greater part of the day is, necessarily, spent travelling. Because of this, overnight stops are quite far apart and the visitor should not linger or spend too much time at any one point along the way.

In the description of the various routes, the suggested roads are often followed by an alphabetical letter and numeral(s) inserted in brackets. For example '. . the tarred road (H1-1) to Pretoriuskop . . .' This code allows the reader to accurately pinpoint the road on a map and avoid uncertainties.

ROUTE 1. Two days. Night stops: Skukuza, Satara

Short Description. DAY 1: Having arrived late the previous afternoon and spent the night in Skukuza, depart early. Day 1 – follow the tarred road (H4-1) to Lower Sabie for breakfast. From there drive via Mlondozi dam (S29 + S68), Orpen dam (S29 + H10 + H1-2 + S32) and Tshokwane picnic-site (H1-2) to Satara (H1-3) in time for lunch. This is followed by an afternoon drive to Nwanedzi lookout point (H1-3 + H6) and back (S41 + S100) to Satara for night stop.

DAY 2: After breakfast use the H1-4 and S90 roads to reach the causeway crossing the Olifants river near Balule camp. From there turn onto S92 for refreshments at Olifants camp. Then follow the river roads (S44 + S93 + S46) to reach Letaba in time for lunch. After lunch use the tarred road (H-9) for a view of Masorini ruins and finally leave the Park at Phalaborwa Gate.

Full Description. The route described below is recommended for visitors who only have a weekend at their disposal.

Most visitors will probably arrive in Skukuza late on Friday afternoon. In such cases the evening could be spent viewing the exhibits in the Stevenson-Hamilton Library or watching the open-air wild-life film-shows in the amphitheatre in front of the library.

Try to leave Skukuza as early as possible on Saturday morning (or Day 1), preferably as soon as the camp gates are opened. As well as being more successful, game-viewing is far more pleasant in the early morning. Very often the first few cars to leave camp will find lions lying on the road.

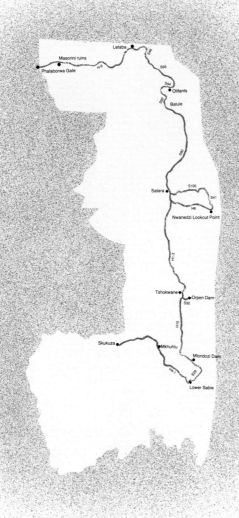

Letaba
S46
Masorini ruins
S93
H-9
Phalaborwa Gate
S44
Olifants
S90
Balule

S90

S100
Satara
S41
H6
Nwanedzi Lookout Point

H1-3

Tshokwane
Orpen Dam
S32

H10

Skukuza
Mkhuhlu
Mlondozi Dam
H4-1
S29
Lower Sabie

Follow the tarred road (H4-1) along the river to Lower Sabie camp which you should reach in time for breakfast. This drive is well-known for the abundance of impala, kudu, warthog, baboon, vervet monkeys and several other species, and the very good possibility of finding lion and leopard. Short drives off the main road take one close to the river where crocodiles can often be seen.

After breakfast, cross the Sabie river causeway using the H10 road. Keep to this road for about a kilometre, then turn off onto the S29 which leads to Mlondozi dam. Follow the road up to the hill-top lookout point where covered seating provides an excellent view of the dam and a vast surrounding area. Hippo and crocodile share the dam with a large number of birds such as ducks, herons, kingfishers and storks, while kudu, waterbuck, impala and occasionally elephant approach the bank for water or to feed on the nearby vegetation. There are toilets at the lookout point and cool drinks can be bought.

From Mlondozi dam drive back along the S29 to rejoin the H10 heading for Tshokwane. Two kilometres before reaching Tshokwane the road links with the tarred road (H1-2) from Skukuza. Roughly one kilometre further north, turn off onto the road (S32) to Orpen dam. From your hill-top position at the dam you can observe many crocodiles on the banks, while nearby occasional herds of impala, waterbuck and other animals warily drink their fill. Occasionally elephant arrive, irritably scattering the crocodiles before quenching their thirst. Toilets are next to the parking area.

Having doubled-back along the S32 to Tshokwane again, tea, coffee or other refreshments can be enjoyed at this lovely picnic-site on a quaint verandah built around the base of a huge sausage tree.

From Tshokwane drive northwards again on the tarred road (H1-3) which for a considerable distance hugs the normally dry Nwaswitsontso stream before shearing away to continue through the grassy plains stretching as far as the eye can see. Along the way Mazithi and Kumana dams are passed, where herds of zebra, wildebeest, impala, kudu and waterbuck are common in summer. Lions are abundant on this road.

Budget your time so that Satara is reached for an early lunch. Before eating, check in at the reception office to find out where your hut is. The office is closed between 1 and 2 p.m. so that checking in first avoids an unnecessary wait.

While travelling between Skukuza, Lower Sabie and Satara you could expect to see, on average, the following number of herds or groups of animals: baboon (4); buffalo (2); bushbuck (2); duiker (1); elephant (2); giraffe (8); hippo (2); impala (73); kudu (15); lion (1); steenbok (3); vervet monkey (4); warthog (8); waterbuck (5); wildebeest (5); zebra (8).

After lunch at Satara, and a possible short rest or stroll around camp, you can look forward to a particularly pleasant drive. Take the tarred road (H1-3) out of camp again towards Tshokwane, but turn off after about three kilometres onto the tarred road (H6) to Nwanedzi.

Do not be disappointed if you don't see much on the way to Nwanedzi – it is the return drive which will make the afternoon's trip worthwhile. Even so, the short journey to Nwanedzi should result in sightings of several herds of zebra, wildebeest, impala, and perhaps some ostriches.

Nwanedzi camp is out of bounds except to visitors actually staying there, so go straight to the Nwanedzi lookout point. Here you will find a setting so beautiful that it will long be remembered as one of the most pleasant sights of your visit to the Park. The thatch-roofed lookout point with ample seating stands on the very edge of a sheer cliff which drops to the calm, crystal-clear waters of the Sweni river. Innumerable bright green lily-pads drape the surface of the water. To the west the sun-baked plains roll ever-onwards to the horizon; to the east the rock-littered craggy heights of the Lebombo mountains loom silently aloof. Animals can be seen coming for an afternoon drink and water-birds are abundant.

From the Nwanedzi lookout point take the gravel road (S41) north, then turn off onto the S100 which travels along the Nwanedzi river back towards Satara. This pleasant drive provides great scenic views and many animals. Where the road runs close to the river storks, herons and ducks complement the tranquil water, while waterbuck, zebra, wildebeest, impala and kudu are common. Lion, elephant, buffalo and leopard are often seen along this road. Eventually the tarred road (H1-3) is joined again immediately south of Satara. From there, back to camp to relax.

During the afternoon's drive to Nwanedzi and back to Satara you could expect to have seen the following number of herds or groups of animals: baboon (2); buffalo (1); elephant (1); giraffe (2); impala (17); kudu (6); steenbok (2); warthog (2); waterbuck (5); wildebeest (10); zebra (6). Most of these animals will be seen on the return drive.

After an early breakfast in Satara on Day 2 (try to be on the road by 7.45 a.m.), take the tarred road (H1-4) north towards Olifants camp. After roughly seven kilometres turn off onto the gravel road (S90). This will take you through flat open country with some waterholes close to the road where plains-loving zebra and wildebeest predominate. Lion, elephant and cheetah may also be seen. When nearing Balule camp you will cross the Hlahleni stream, its banks overgrown by tall jackal berry and apple leaf trees. Watch for water-birds at this point and for leopard which may be resting on a branch in one of the trees.

Soon after passing Balule camp the road crosses the Olifants river to fork in opposite directions on the north bank. Turn right onto the S92 which rejoins the tarred road (H8) just before Olifants camp.

At Olifants you have time for tea or coffee and refreshments. In front of the restaurant/reception office/shop complex is an observation area which offers a magnificent view of the Olifants river and surrounding bush. You will propably want to spend a little time here.

From Olifants several roads lead to Letaba. Of these the best for scenery and game-viewing are those which meander close to the rivers and offer the opportunity of seeing many bird species found only in close association with water. To reach Letaba therefore, use the gravel road (S44) which turns off the tarred road (H8) about one kilometre out from Olifants camp.

As you progress along this road, the vegetation changes rapidly to mixed mopane veld until, about half-way to Letaba, mopane trees vastly outnumber all other species. The very rare Sharpes' grysbok is sometimes seen along this drive. Near the junction of the S44 with the S93 the road passes close to a hill covered with large boulders; klipspringers are often seen standing in statue-like postures atop these rocks.

After joining the S93 gravel road, continue onwards to link with the S46. Both these roads keep close to the Letaba river so that animals drinking or feeding along the edges are commonly seen. Lion are also often found in this area.

At Letaba you can lunch in the large restaurant which overlooks the river. Elephant often have a long refreshing drink or browse on the vegetation-covered banks in full view.

On the drive from Satara to Letaba via Olifants you may reasonably expect to have seen the following number of herds or groups of animals: buffalo (1); elephant (1); giraffe (4); hippo (2); impala (25); klipspringer (1); kudu (2); warthog (2); wildebeest (2); zebra (8).

From Letaba the closest exit gate is at Phalaborwa. Following the tarred road (H9), a visit to the Masorini ruins about nine kilometres before reaching Phalaborwa Gate is highly recommended. Archaeological research on and around the boulder-pocked hill has revealed fragments and remnants of man's presence here since the late Stone Age. A guide carrying tape-recorded explanations will conduct you up the hill through reconstructions of the huts and living areas used by people of the Iron Age. At the base of the hill a display hut is crammed with archaeological paraphernalia collected here and at other sites. Toilets are situated at the parking area, and cool drinks are available.

From there on through the exit gate to the nearby town of Phalaborwa where an airport has flights to Johannesburg's Jan Smuts Airport (find out the departure times beforehand). There are Avis branches in town and at the airport.

ROUTE 2. Three days. Night stops: Skukuza, Lower Sabie, Satara.

Short Description. DAY 1. Having arrived in the Park late the previous afternoon and spent the night in Skukuza, depart early. Day 1 – follow the tarred road (H1-1) for breakfast at Pretoriuskop. Then drive via Jock-of-the-Bushveld road (H2-2) – possibly stopping at the Afsaal picnic-site – and Crocodile Bridge (S25) to Lower Sabie (S28) for overnight stop.

DAY 2. After breakfast drive via Mlondozi dam (S29 + S68), Orpen dam (S29 + H10 + H1-2 + S32) and Tshokwane picnic-site (H1-2) to

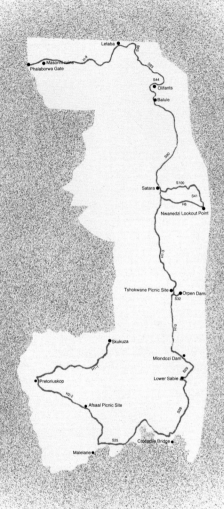

Letaba

Masorini Ruins
Phalaborwa Gate

H9

S46

S93

S44

Olifants
Balule

S90

S100

Satara
S41

H6

Nwanedzi Lookout Point

H1-3

Tshokwane Picnic Site
S32

Orpen Dam

H10

Skukuza

Miondozi Dam

H1-1

S29

Pretoriuskop

Lower Sabie

H2-2

Afsaal Picnic Site

S28

S25

Crocodile Bridge

Malelane

Satara (H1-3) in time for lunch. This is followed by an afternoon drive to Nwanedzi lookout point (H1-3 + H6) and back to Satara (S41 + S100) for the night.

DAY 3. After breakfast follow the H1-4 and S90 roads to reach the causeway crossing the Olifants river near Balule camp. From there turn onto S92 for refreshments at Olifants camp. Follow the river roads (S44 + S93 + S46) to reach Letaba for lunch. After lunch use the tarred road (H-9) for a view of the Masorini ruins and to leave the Park at Phalaborwa Gate.

Full Description. If three days are at your disposal, a long weekend for example, the following route is suggested. Again it is assumed that arrival in Skukuza, where the first night is spent, will be late in the afternoon. The evening may be spent over a leisurely dinner in the restaurant, exploring the Stevenson-Hamilton Library, watching one of the open-air film-shows, or simply lounging on the restaurant verandah where drinks are served.

Leave Skukuza as early as possible the next morning, Day 1, following the tarred road (H1-1) to Pretoriuskop. Wild-dogs, lion and rhino are frequently seen on this road and the scenery is pleasant. With luck, a rare klipspringer may be seen on the rocky hills which jut out close to the road roughly 14 kilometres from Skukuza. Further along, it may be worthwhile to turn off briefly to Shitlhave dam, where a few animals could be arriving for their first drink of the day. Don't stay too long however, as a fairly heavy day's driving and several dams or watering-points still lie ahead.

Breakfast at Pretoriuskop, and then take the Jock-of-the-Bushveld road (H2-2) towards the Afsaal picnic site, where light refreshments are available. Ship mountain, so called because from a distance it is supposed to resemble the inverted hull of a ship, is passed about 13 kilometres out of Pretoriuskop. It is a mass of boulders unlike other hills in the vicinity, and lies in an area favoured by rhino.

The first section of the road towards Malelane leads through rather dense bushveld of medium-sized silver terminalias, shrub-like sickle-bush, a wide range of larger but less abundant trees and a thick carpet of thatching-grass which in places reaches two metres high. The vegetation changes almost imperceptibly until, near Malelane, tall lead-wood, marula, knobthorn, acacias, and smaller bush-willows become more abundant. The drive is never boring as game is plentiful and the road twists and winds through interesting country.

You will not be able to enter Malelane as it is a private camp, so continue along the Crocodile river road (S25) to Crocodile Bridge. About five kilometres before reaching Crocodile Bridge a well-marked road (S27) leads off to a hippo-pool in the Crocodile River. A herd of hippo have made their home here and spend much of their day lazing on a sand-bank in open view. Elephant and other animals often come down to drink so, with luck, these may also be seen. A Bushman painting adorns the rock-cliff which overlooks the hippo-pool.

Try to budget your time so that a maximum of 2,5 hours is spent on the trip from Pretoriuskop to the turn off onto the S25 road near Malelane, and similarly no more than 2,5 hours from that point to Crocodile Bridge.

After a cool drink and walk around the camp at Crocodile Bridge, follow the Nhlowa road (S28) to Lower Sabie. There is an alternate tarred road, but the S28, besides being a little shorter, leads to the Mhlanganzwane dam where a range of animal species is sure to be seen at this time of day. Allowing about two hours for this trip, Lower Sabie should be reached by 3.30 p.m., leaving ample time for tea and a snack, checking into the reception office, and unloading baggage into your reserved accommodation.

The drive from Skukuza to Lower Sabie via Pretoriuskop and Crocodile Bridge is one of the most pleasant and rewarding in the entire Park. The scenery is absorbing and animals abound. During the trip you can expect to see, on average, the following number of herds or groups of animals: baboon (3); buffalo (1); duiker (2); elephant (1); giraffe (5); hippo (1); hyena (1); impala (90); jackal (1); kudu (5); lion (1); steenbok (4); vervet monkey (2); warthog (11); waterbuck (1); wildebeest (4); zebra (5).

For the remaining two days i.e. Day 2 and Day 3, the same route from Lower Sabie as described under Route 1 is recommended.

ROUTE 3. Five days. Overnight stops: Skukuza, Lower Sabie, Satara, Letaba, Punda Maria.

Short Description. DAY 1. Having arrived in the Park late the previous afternoon and spent the night in Skukuza, depart early. Day 1 – follow the tarred road (H1-1) to Pretoriuskop for breakfast. Then drive via Jock-of-the-Bushveld road (H2-2) and Crocodile Bridge (S25) to Lower Sabie (S28) for an overnight stop.

DAY 2. After breakfast drive via Mlondozi dam (S29 + S68), Orpen dam (S29 + H10 + H1-2 + S32) and Tshokwane picnic-site (H1-2) to Satara (H1-3) for lunch. This is followed by an afternoon drive to Nwanedzi lookout point (H1-3 + H6) and back (S41 + S100) to Satara for the night.

DAY 3. After breakfast use H1-4 and S90 roads to reach the causeway crossing the Olifants river near Balule camp. From there turn onto S92 for refreshments at Olifants camp. Follow the river roads (S44 + S93 + S46) to reach Letaba for lunch. After lunch follow the H1-6 tarred road and S48 gravel road to Mingerhout dam on the Letaba river, followed by the drive back along the river (S47) and tarred road (H1-6) to Letaba camp for the night.

DAY 4. After breakfast follow the tarred road (H1-6) north and eventually turn off onto the gravel road (S50) heading past Shawu dam to Shingwedzi. Nearing the Kanniedood dam the road changes in designation to S51; continue along it past Kanniedood dam to Shingwedzi for lunch. The afternoon is taken up by the drive to Punda Maria for a

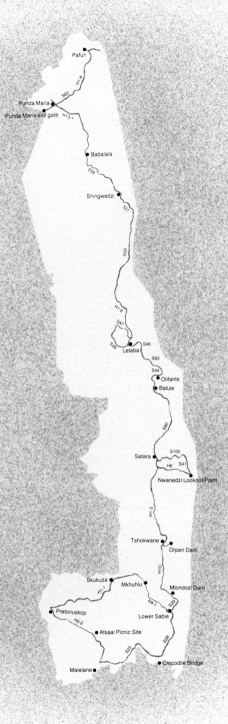

Pafuri

Punda Maria
Punda Maria exit gate

Babalala

Shingwedzi

Letaba

Olifants
Balule

Satara

Nwanedzi Lookout Point

Tshokwane
Orpen Dam

Skukuza
Mkhuhlu
Mlondozi Dam

Pretoriuskop
Lower Sabie

Afsaal Picnic Site

Malelane
Crocodile Bridge

night stop, following H1-7, S56, H1-7, H13-1, and H13-2 roads.

DAY 5. The morning is taken up by a drive to the unique Pafuri area, following H13-2, S60, S61, H1-8, S63, and S64 roads. Then back along the same roads to join the S98 near Punda Maria, leaving the Park at the gate 10 km south-west of Punda Maria camp.

Full Description. Five days are about the absolute minimum time needed to gain a fair impression of what the Park has to offer in scenery and animals, and to absorb some of its character and atmosphere. For those having five days available, a suggested route is:

For the first three full days follow Route 2, already described, but instead of leaving the Park at the Phalaborwa Gate after lunch at Letaba on day 3, check in at the Letaba reception office.

During the afternoon take a circular drive along the H1-6 tarred road and S48 gravel road to the Mingerhout dam where a lookout point provides an excellent view of the Letaba river. Hippopotamuses usually move about in the dam, while below the spillway several crocodiles sun themselves on the sandy shores. Water-birds are common.

On the way back to Letaba, the S47 gravel road remains close to the river. It is a pleasant drive through good scenery which should enable you to see elephant, zebra, impala and waterbuck along with a range of birds such as storks, ducks, herons and darters. The tarred road (H1-6) is joined about five kilometres from Letaba camp. Turn left for a good view of the river from the bridge where you are also likely to see hippo, elephant, or buffalo. Then back to Letaba camp for the night.

After breakfast at Letaba on day 4 follow the tarred road (H1-6) north towards Shingwedzi. Five kilometres after leaving camp you cross the Letaba river where several hippo will probably be sunning themselves on a sand-bank.

Driving on, the scenery differs strikingly from that of the south. Vast stretches of seemingly endless mopane scrub-land roll from horizon to horizon, broken only by herds of zebra, wildebeest, impala, tsessebe and elephant.

About 27 kilometres after crossing the Letaba river bridge, a gravel road (S50) turns off to the right, heading for the Lebombo mountains. This road will take you past several dams and streams where zebra, jmpala, tsessebe, elephant and waterbuck are common. At the Shawu dam water-birds line the banks and dot the dead trees.

Further north the road again veers westwards towards Shingwedzi, following the river of the same name. Eventually you will reach the Kanniedood dam, a magnificent expanse of water with many water-birds and animals in the vicinity. Darters are exceptionally abundant and pose breathtakingly on the logs and rocks which rise from the water surface.

A few kilometres on you will reach Shingwedzi camp for a much-needed break after the long drive from Letaba. A leisurely lunch and stroll around camp should relax the legs and any aching backs.

The final stretch to Punda Maria follows the H1-7 tarred road. There is a gravel road (S56) which travels along the Mphongolo river through beautiful groves of tall nyala, jackal berry and apple leaf trees which form a welcome relief from the mopane plains dominating the northern half of the Park. This gravel road turns off the H1-7 about eight kilometres from Shingwedzi and rejoins it at Babalala picnic-site. Here you may want to get out for a short walk, but there are seldom animals to be seen around the vegetation-filled marshland which crowds close to the picnic-site.

Continue on the tarred road (H1-7) for 27 kilometres when another tarred road (H13-1) turns off to the left. This road links with the H13-2 which will take you to your overnight stop at Punda Maria. This is a small rustic camp with tremendous atmosphere and character.

Travelling between Letaba and Punda Maria, using the roads described, the following number of herds or groups of animals can reasonably be expected to be seen: baboon (2); buffalo (1); elephant (2); giraffe (1); hippo (1); impala (20); kudu (3); nyala (1); steenbok (2); tsessebe (2); warthog (2); waterbuck (8); wildebeest (1); zebra (8).

On the final day a drive to the Pafuri area on the S60 and S61 gravel roads and the H1-8 tarred road is highly recommended. Initially you drive through dense forests of tall mopane trees which eventually give way to the now familiar mopane-scrub plains where baobabs and low hills become increasingly frequent.

Finally the Luvuvhu river with its lush riverine forest is reached. Following the S64 and S63 river drives you are certain to see graceful and stately nyala, and perhaps bushbuck which are very beautiful but tend to disappear into the undergrowth soon after being spotted. Baboons and monkeys are numerous and the bird-life is exceptional. Crested guinea-fowl are occasionally seen, and the eerie sounds of trumpeter hornbills and fish eagles calling are almost certain to be heard.

At the Pafuri picnic-site, where hot water and toilets are available, trumpeter hornbills often rest in the huge fig trees dominating the riverside. With a little luck a fish eagle may be observed from the bridge crossing the Luvuvhu river. Hippos are likely to be found, either at the bridge or along the river drives. The unique scenery alone is well worth the trip.

No facilities are available for buying food at Pafuri so it is wise to take a prepared lunch, enjoying it at the Pafuri picnic-site.

Follow the same route back to Punda Maria, leaving the Kruger Park at the exit gate a few kilometres south-west of the camp. The road continues through the Republic of Venda to Louis Trichardt, Pietersburg, Pretoria and Johannesburg. No documents are required to pass through Venda.

The trip to and around Pafuri on the final day should result in the following number of herds or groups of animals being seen: baboon (4); bushbuck (1); hippo (1); impala (13); kudu (1); nyala (2); vervet monkey (3); warthog (2); waterbuck (1); zebra (1).

Literature consulted

Annual Reports, Kruger National Park. 1960-1961 to 1981-1982.

CODD, L.E.W. 1951. **Trees and Shrubs of the Kruger National Park.** Botanical survey memoir no. 26. Union of South Africa Department of Agriculture. Government Printer, Pretoria.

DALY, H.V., DOYEN, J.T. and EHRLICH, P.R. 1978. **Introduction to insect biology and diversity.** McGraw-Hill, Johannesburg.

HANKS, J. 1980. **Mammals of Southern Africa.** McGraw-Hill, Johannesburg.

KLOPPERS, J., and VAN SON, G. 1978. **Butterflies of the Kruger National Park.** National Parks Board of Curators, Pretoria.

LABUSCHAGNE, R.J., and VAN DER MERWE, N.J. 1971. **Mammals of the Kruger and other National Parks.** National Parks Board of Trustees.

MARSHALL, A.J., and WILLIAMS, W.D. 1974. **Textbook of Zoology, Invertebrates.** Macmillan Press, London.

McLACHLAN, G.R., and LIVERSIDGE, R. 1978. **Roberts Birds of South Africa.** Trustees of the John Voelcker Bird Book Fund, Cape Town.

NEWMAN, K. 1980. **Birds of Southern Africa 1. Kruger National Park.** Macmillan, Johannesburg.

PIENAAR, U. DE V. 1980. **The Reptile Fauna of the Kruger National Park.** National Parks Board of Trustees, Pretoria.

PIENAAR, U. DE V., PASSMORE, N.I., and CARRUTHERS, V.C. 1976. **The Frogs of the Kruger National Park.** National Parks Board of Trustees, Pretoria.

PIENAAR, U. DE V., RAUTENBACH, I.L., and DE GRAAFF, G. 1980. **The Small Mammals of the Kruger National Park.** National Parks Board of Trustees, Pretoria.

SKAIFE, S.H., LEDGER, J., and BANNISTER, A. 1979. **African Insect Life.** C. Struik, Cape Town.

STEVENSON-HAMILTON, J. 1947. **South African Eden.** Collins, London.

VAN DER SPUY, U. 1971. **Wild Flowers of South Africa for the Garden.** Keartland, Johannesburg.

VAN WYK, P. 1972. **Trees of the Kruger National Park.** (Two volumes.) Purnell, Cape Town.

YATES, J.H. 1968. **Spiders of SouthernAfrica.** Books of Africa, Cape Town.

Checklists

Below is a listing of some of the mammals, birds and trees you can expect to see during your visit and the pages on which entries concerning them appear. Next to each is a series of boxes; use only the first one for marking off each species seen on this trip, the other boxes can be used on future visits to the Park. In this way you can compare the relative 'viewing success' of each trip.

Mammals

Baboon (Chacma baboon) 84
Banded mongoose 67
Black-backed jackal 65
Black rhinoceros 70
Blue wildebeest 83
Buffalo 73
Burchell's zebra 82
Bushbuck 77
Caracal 67
Cheetah 63
Civet cat 66
Duiker (common or grey duiker) 76
Dwarf mongoose 68
Eland 80
Elephant 68
Genet 67
Giraffe 83
Grysbok (Sharpe's grysbok) 76
Hippopotamus 73
Hyena (spotted hyena) 65
Impala 75
Jackal (black-backed jackal) 65
Klipspringer 76
Kudu 83
Leopard 62
Lion 60
Mongoose, Banded 67
Mongoose, Dwarf 68
Monkey (vervet monkey) 85
Nyala 78
Rhinoceros, Black 70
Rhinoceros, White 70
Roan antelope 79
Sable antelope 80
Serval 67
Sharpe's grysbok 76
Spotted hyena 65
Steenbok 75
Tsessebe 80
Vervet monkey 85
Warthog 86
Waterbuck 79
White rhinoceros 70
Wild cat 67
Wild-dog 64
Wildebeest (Blue wildebeest) 83
Zebra (Burchell's zebra) 82

Birds

Bee-eaters 104
    Carmine bee-eater 104
    European bee-eater 104
    Little bee-eater 104
    White-fronted bee-eater 104
Black Crake 97
Bulbuls 107
    Black-eyed bulbul 107
Bustard (kori bustard) 100
Darter 88
Dikkops 99
    Spotted dikkop 99
    Water dikkop 99
Doves 100
    Cape turtle dove 100
    Emerald-spotted dove 100
    Laughing dove 100
    Red-eyed turtle dove 100
Ducks 91
    Knob-billed duck 92
    White-faced duck 91
Eagles 95
    Bateleur 96
    Brown snake eagle 96
    Fish eagle 95
    Martial eagle 96
    Tawny eagle 96